Questions And Observations On The Conflict Between Faith-Based and Secular Rationalities

Joseph E. Keysor

Published by Joseph E. Keysor, 2023.

QUESTIONS AND OBSERVATIONS ON THE CONFLICT BETWEEN FAITH-BASED AND SECULAR RATIONALITIES

First edition. March 24, 2023.

Copyright © 2023 Joseph E. Keysor.

ISBN: 979-8215469163

Written by Joseph E. Keysor.

Also by Joseph E. Keysor

Light in the Darkness of Postmodernism: An American Christian
Surveys His Life and Times

Questions And Observations On The Conflict Between Faith-Based
and Secular Rationalities

Where is the American Church? Three Essays on Salvation, Sin and
Judgment

Table of Contents

Preface

If an atheist reasons from the assumptions that "There is no God," and "There is no immortal soul or spirit, or any kind of non-material essence that abides after physical death," he is reasoning from assumptions that have never been empirically demonstrated in the laboratory or independently confirmed in various places by repeated and controlled experiments. That is, his scientific reasoning has an unscientific starting point.

Conversely, if a theist reasons from the assumptions that "God exists," and "Our immortal souls will appear before him after death to be judged," the non-scientific nature of his assumptions does not mean that he is totally irrational. To think, "I am going to be judged by God so I should do this, but I should not do that" is rational, and logical, if God exists. To think that "God created us, and therefore we find our highest fulfilment by living in harmony with God's laws" is not at all irrational, if God exists.

Thus we can say these two different rationalities, which we may call "secular" and "faith-based," are not separated by a sort of metaphysical Berlin Wall, an impassible barrier defended by barbed wire, minefields, guard dogs and machine guns. People can use reason in religious or non-religious contexts, with often conflicting results even when operating from shared beliefs or assumptions. Parenthetically, rather than trying to take all of the many different varieties of theism into account, I have tried to discuss this issue from the standpoint of belief in the 66 books of the Old and New Testaments, in a generally Protestant context (though the Reformation was centuries ago, and I am not currently protesting anything).

This does not mean there are different rationalities when it comes to physics, chemistry, engineering, and so on. On the material plane, facts are facts. It is on the higher and remoter levels of cosmic origins, meaning, purpose and ethics that different yet plausible approaches to reality enter in. This problem is compounded by the fact that "rationality" and "reason" are both often slippery and highly subjective terms. If a criminal wants to avoid detection, concealing the evidence is a rational thing to do. If a dictator wants to invade a neighboring country, building up his military while lulling the neighbor into a false sense of security is a rational thing to do.

Given the complexity of the debate between two conflicting views of the world – spiritual and theistic, vs. materialistic and atheistic – it seems worthwhile to try and clarify the boundaries between them. Particularly important in this regard are the social consequences. If there is or is not a God, if there are or are not higher principles or even divinely instituted laws we need to follow to maximize human flourishing, these are not merely abstract topics for philosophical hobbyists. They affect us directly in every aspect of life.

Particular attention has been given in some parts of this essay to the issue or question of Protestant theological liberalism. The phenomenon of a secular mindset seeking comfort in a security blanket of religious language (which originated primarily in 19th-century Germany) has caused a great deal of confusion. When words like "salvation . . . sin . . . God . . . God's word . . . heaven" and so on appear, one can hardly be blamed for assuming that this is religious. However, when the basic truth and particular truths of the Bible are denied; when the deity of Christ, the virgin birth, the reality of a day of judgment followed by heaven or hell are denied, and the aforementioned words are defined according to human reason alone – then what we have is in effect a sort of religious humanism, a spirit of independence from God's laws dressed up in religious clothing.

Underneath all of this is the essential, primary, basic and fundamental question: "Does God exist?" If God does not exist, then the theists are deceived (though many of their ideas an attitudes on specific questions may still be right, because of our shared human nature and common reason). If, on the other hand, God does exist, then it is the theists who are deceived (though many of their ideas an attitudes on specific questions may still be right, because of our shared human nature and common reason).

This all-important question is not answered on the basis of laboratory experiments, microscopic or telescopic observations and/or mathematical calculations. It is answered on the basis of highly personal and subjective factors, usually not clearly known by the individual subjects themselves. In facing these two alternative answers we have need of reason, logic, evidence and facts, but we also need something more than merely detached objectivity.

Intelligence alone is inadequate here. We need a spirit of humility, a consciousness that our minds are weak and feeble relative to the great mysteries of life and the cosmos. We need a spirit of detachment and self-denial, since the underlying ground of all reality is most certainly not something that conforms to all of our expectations and desires. We need a certain human transcendence of the pains and pleasures of the world, even as we remain in the world.

We need to be prepared to change our ways if need be, to admit we are wrong if need be, if we want to escape from the self-imposed tyranny that limits our thoughts and conclusions to mere personal preference. This requires a certain dying to self, which is never easy or pleasant. For this reason Jesus Christ said, "For whosoever will save his life shall lose it." He also said, "Ask, and it shall be given you; seek, and ye shall find; knock, and it shall be opened unto you: For every one that asketh receiveth; and he that seeketh findeth; and to him that knocketh it shall be opened."

73 Questions and Observations

Given the vast amounts of anti-religious arguments, propaganda and sometimes even ridicule that have been directed against religious belief in general and the Christian religion in particular, it seemed worthwhile, and in the interest of truth, to present some alternative arguments. "Come now, and let us reason together," said the prophet Isaiah in the 8th century BC, though the words immediately following after "reason together" are "says the Lord." This means it was God himself inviting to us to reason with Him. But here, we humans can reason among ourselves, for which purpose I offer up the following thoughts.

1. When scientists say "God does not exist," they are speaking outside of their fields of expertise. Hence, it should be recognized that their opinions or beliefs on the subject are no more valid or authoritative than anyone else's. This is true regardless of whatever prestige they might have acquired through scientific endeavor.

2. Those who deny the existence of God are not expressing scientific fact that is necessarily derived from a detached consideration of empirical evidence. They are merely expressing their own understanding based on personal and emotional as well as on intellectual factors.

3. To deny the existence of God and assert that the universe and our world all came into being by blind chance is not automatically rational. It is only rational if there is no God. If there is a God, it is highly and deeply irrational, and contrary to human flourishing on the highest levels.

4. Many people have idiosyncratic definitions of "rationality." They arbitrarily draw the boundaries of what is "rational" and "irrational" to fit their own personal preferences.

5. Scientists do not automatically have special insight or wisdom in areas that fall outside of the precise confines of the scientific method. This includes such topics as:

~ the reality of life after death

~ the first emergence of the world and of the cosmos

~ the origin of human and animal life

~ the nature and origin of human ethics

~ the existence or the non-existence of God

~ the reality of biblical miracles

~ the virgin birth of Christ

~ the sacrificial death and resurrection of Christ

~ the resurrection of the dead

~ art, music, philosophy, economics, politics, literature, sports and entertainment

~ ordinary and basic human emotions such as love, hate, happiness, or unhappiness

6. The scientific method is limited to the material world, to matter and to objects subject to human control, manipulation and study. Questions outside of naturalistic boundaries are permanently beyond the reach of meaningful scientific theorizing, hypothesizing, analyzing and predicting.

7. People need to be more skeptical of scientists who seek to enter the public arena and interfere in social, political, philosophical,

religious and moral subjects very far removed from their areas of specialty.

8. Are we basically good people in a fundamentally irrational universe, or are we basically flawed people in a fundamentally rational one?

9. The successes of the scientific method are undeniable. However, it should not be forgotten that the results of applied science have not always been beneficial.

10. Science, through the development of weapons of mass destruction, has confronted planet earth with one of the greatest threats to human flourishing in all of recorded history.

11. Scientists, many of them diligently toiling in obedience to the state, have provided us with many lesser weapons such as napalm, military airplanes, machine guns, rockets, biological weapons, poison gas, and innumerable explosives. Science has helped to make warfare far more destructive than it ever was in the past.

12. Current experiments that consist of creating new and dangerous viruses solely for the sake of some hypothetical knowledge reveal some medical scientists as great sources of danger to the well-being of us all. But, our well-being and flourishing is not their concern.

13. What if there should be a terrorist attack, or an earthquake, fire, or structural defect that should release deadly new viruses on an unsuspecting world? This is much more of a real and present danger than any presented by biblical Christianity – which in fact poses no dangers at all.

14. Advances in medical science have also made possible current abortion practices. It is a profound irony, that one of the greatest areas of scientific benefit – modern medicine – has led to massive social self-destruction, and millions upon millions of unnecessary deaths.

15. If the ages of aborted infants were to be figured into calculations of longevity, average life expectancy might be found to be no more advanced that it was 300 years ago.

16. The social cost of those missing millions who will never grow up to marry, go to school, build, invent, work, and create can never be calculated.

17. We do not have the right to do whatever we want with our own bodies independently of any higher law. "For we must all appear before the judgment seat of Christ; that every one may receive the things done in his body, according to that he hath done, whether it be good or bad."

18. Applied science, in spite of its many benefits, has also been greatly detrimental to human well-being through the proliferation of modern entertainments (junk food for the soul) and modern convenient and fun foods (junk food for the body).

19. The statement "Only that which is verifiable by the scientific method can properly be called knowledge" cannot itself be verified by the scientific method. Therefore, it is not real knowledge, but merely a statement of personal belief.

20. David Hume claimed "If we take in our hand any volume; of divinity or school metaphysics, for instance; let us ask, Does it contain any abstract reasoning concerning quantity or number? No. Does it contain any experimental reasoning concerning matter of fact and existence? No. Commit it then to the flames: for it can contain nothing but sophistry and illusion." Whence did he derive this insight?

21. There are problems with applying the Euthyphro dilemma to God, because God so far transcends us, but when applied to human beings such as Hume, the dilemma is impossible to escape. Where did Hume get the aforementioned insight? Was it solely from within himself? Then it is his personal opinion at best. Was it from an external source of truth? Than what precisely is that source, and how did Hume access it?

22. That the Euthyphro dilemma is a problem for humans but fails to reach as far as God can be explained thusly. Do God's moral judgments come from some other external standard? No, because there is nothing greater than God, who is himself the source of all that exists. Does that mean his judgments are therefore arbitrary in a pejorative human sense, meaning capricious and unreasonable, and hence inadequate as moral standards, because they come solely from himself? No, because while arbitrary human judgments are inherently inadequate due to our limitations and fallibility, the judgments of God are necessarily and inherently right, he being the ultimate source of all that is. His judgements can come solely from himself, yet still be true and valid, and not merely arbitrary in a fallible human sense. This is because of the unchangeable perfection of his being.

23. When Christ said "And fear not them which kill the body, but are not able to kill the soul: but rather fear him which is able to destroy both soul and body in hell," this is an affirmation of body / soul dualism.

24. Mathematical proof does not equal scientific proof, and achieves its results by something other than the scientific method. This discredits naturalistic scientists' claims that theirs alone is the true path to knowledge.

25. If there is one way of knowing that exists outside of the limited parameters of naturalistic science, who is to say there may not be others?

26. Some naturalists' claims are true, but do not tell us how to live, as they are merely descriptive of the material world. Some naturalistic claims are falsehoods, arrived at by methods deeper and more subjective than the bare scientific method.

27. Scientists do not know what sorts of natural laws might be operative in different parts of the universe.

28. Can anyone assert with confidence that the speed of light or the force of gravity in a remote galaxy must be precisely the same as ours?

29. No one has any idea what sort of scientific laws might have been operative and what sort of conditions might have present in the formation of the earth, the solar system, and the cosmos.

30. Cosmological concepts such as string theory, multiverses, baby universes, cosmic evolution, and so on do not even remotely approach authentic science.

31. Secularism has not brought much individual happiness. It does not stimulate the deepest and highest dimensions of the mind or of the soul.

32. Scriptural Christianity, with its emphasis on a higher meaning and purpose of life, does more to develop the human soul on its deepest levels than does the belief that we are basically animals, existing for no good reason in a silent and impersonal universe.

33. It is the eternal truths of the existence of God, the immortality of the soul, and the need to live in service and obedience to God that guide the soul to a higher level of flourishing – if, that is, they are animated and instructed by the Spirit and by the mind of Christ.

34. A correct understanding of human happiness, what it is and how to achieve it, depends on a correct understanding of human origins. If we came about as the result of blind chance and the random operations of matter and energy, a correct concept of happiness and the good life must necessarily be different than it would be if we were created by a divine power for some higher purpose.

35. Our understanding of freedom, goodness or virtue, as well as our attitudes toward life and death vary greatly according to our understanding of the primary question of the existence of God.

36. Atheism in the end involves much more than a mere denial of God's existence. Human nature being what it is, our concepts of the existence or the non-existence of God inevitably influence our understanding of other aspects of life.

37. Do our hazy and divergent concepts of ethics and of right and wrong have their origins in a divine creation, which sets us apart from

all other living species on earth? Or is our sense of right and wrong merely the inexplicable result of an impersonal Darwinian process in which the weaker and the less fit perish?

38. Explanations should be adequate to the effects they seek to explain. If Darwinism cannot explain music, a sense of humor, love, and numerous other human emotions and character traits, then it is not an adequate explanation for the existence of mankind.

39. According to Darwinism, wasn't the displacement of the American Indians by the Europeans merely an example of survival of the fittest?

40. It is not possible that some atheists may be right and others may be wrong on the question of the existence of God, since they all must agree that God does not exist – if at least we accept the common dictionary definition of an atheist.

41. It is possible that some theists may be right and others may be wrong about God, as they may have widely divergent views as to his nature.

42. If it takes a significant amount of time and effort to learn a foreign language or master a musical instrument, how much more time might it take to come to a deeper and truer understanding of life and of God, the ultimate source of all that is?

43. Those who say that religion is the primary cause of violence in the world, or even just a significant cause, are (a) ignoring the contrary evidence of millions of Christians who live peaceful lives harming no one, and (b) ignoring or at least drastically minimizing the vast amounts of violence that have been and are being committed by people of all sorts for non-religious reasons.

44. America did not go to war in Vietnam because of religion. Napoleon did not invade Italy, Spain, Belgium, Russia and other countries because of religion. The Romans, the Vikings, the Mongols, the Huns were not driven by religious considerations. The English

occupation of Ireland began centuries before the Protestant Reformation.

45. The greatest source of violence in America today, including not merely individual crimes but also massive outbreaks of organized looting and violence, is not people who are trying to follow the teachings of Jesus Christ as closely as possible.

46. Great increases in urban crime are not caused by people who believe in the literal truth of the Bible. They are caused by people who do not care about God's laws or about the possibility of their being held accountable on a future day of judgment.

47. In Communist China and in the Soviet Union, Christians believers were the victims of consistent and systematic violence and oppression inflicted on them by atheists, for atheistic motives.

48. People who harp on religious violence while ignoring much greater - and much more recent - secular violence, are either misinformed, or else are willfully deceiving people by stating what they know to be false in order to further their own agendas.

49. Atheists who point to the murder of an abortion doctor by an alleged Christian as a proof of the danger of religious belief, while saying nothing about the countless millions of people slain by the secular and militantly atheistic ideology of Communism, are: (a) incapable of objectively considering the facts that lie in plain sight before them, or (b) willfully deceiving people by stating what they know to be false in order to further their own agendas.

50. It was the modernist denial of the Judeo-Christian God as defined in the Old and the New Testaments of the Bible that opened the door to the emergence of such ideological nightmares as Communism, National Socialism, and Fascism. These were far worse than the Inquisition or the Crusades.

51. Modern secular ideologies, whether atheistic (Communism) or vaguely theistic (National Socialism) were predicated upon the falsehood and the irrelevance of biblical teachings.

52. Atheistical concepts of a meaningless cosmos have contributed greatly to the breakdown of modern society by undermining the rule of law, both in the abstract and in social practice.

53. Human nature is inherently fallen and sinful. Therefore, rather than being basically good, people are basically sinful and are themselves the sources of many of the evils that plague this troubled world.

54. This being so, we can expect to find sinful practices and wrong attitudes among theists and atheists alike. Those who assert or deny the existence of God are alike vulnerable to ignorance and error, as well as to misguided and harmful passions. Sin has both religious and secular manifestations.

55. The events of the French Revolution, the Russian Revolution, and the Third Reich were all nourished and driven by irreligious ideas and rationalized by human logic operating consistently from false premises.

56. If the nobility must be exterminated to bring about a just society, it is rational to kill them. If the middle classes and the rich are enemies of a revolution that will finally bring in human happiness, it is rational to eliminate them. If the perishing of the unfit facilitates the evolutionary advancement of the human race, then it is rational to expedite the process.

57. The ungodly beliefs that there is no fundamental law in the universe, and that we will never be held accountable in the next life for what we do in this one, are also powerful encouragements to individual acts of violence and crime.

58. Religiously motivated violence is directly contrary to the teachings of Christ. Those who commit it are guilty of sin.

59. Atheistic and rationally motivated violence is directly contrary to nothing fixed and certain. Those who commit it are absolved if their intentions are good.

60. The soul lives after death. There will be a resurrection from the dead, and we will each of us as individuals be held accountable for

the actions, words, intentions and even secret thoughts of our lives. "Marvel not at this: for the hour is coming, in the which all that are in the graves shall hear his voice, And shall come forth; they that have done good, unto the resurrection of life; and they that have done evil, unto the resurrection of damnation."

61. The greatest secular thinkers of the modern era – Mill, Camus, Hume, Kant, Hegel, Sartre, Marx, Nietzsche, Darwin, etc. – were all of them ignorant of this truth, and hence were lost and blind, groping in darkness. Their teachings are delusion, deception and vanity.

62. Scriptural Christianity does not only teach forgiveness of sins and eternal life. It also teaches that a profound renovation of the human personality is not only possible but essential, as we are brought into greater conformity to the reality of the Lord Jesus Christ.

63. Not everyone who has the name or outward appearance of a Christian is guaranteed of a place in heaven.

64. There are many professing Christians who will be rejected on the day of judgment. As Christ said: "Not every one that saith unto me, Lord, Lord, shall enter into the kingdom of heaven; but he that doeth the will of my Father which is in heaven."

65. If done with love and sensitivity, introducing children to basic concepts of right and wrong derived from God provides the possibility of a real foundation for ethics.

66. What contributes most to human flourishing - material prosperity? physical security and safety? amusements and entertainments? physical pleasures?

67. All of those things pass away. To truly find our place in the cosmos we need eternal, abiding and unchanging truths.

68. Christ said, "whosoever drinketh of the water that I shall give him shall never thirst; but the water that I shall give him shall be in him a well of water springing up into everlasting life."

69. The fundamental teachings of Christianity cannot be proven or disproven by science. They are revealed by faith, which is a gift of God granted to some but not to all.

70. It does not follow that the truths of faith are unreal, because they are outside the boundaries of science. It means that science's inherent limitations prevent it from ever coming even close to a comprehensive description of reality, of life, of human consciousness, of vice and virtue, good and evil, righteousness and sin.

71. The common boast that science has made us more humble is nothing but an error at best, and outright deception at worst.

72. Those who sincerely believed that the earth was at the center of the solar system but that they were subject to a higher divine authority were capable of greater and deeper humility than those who know that the earth revolves around the sun but recognize no higher master than their own desires and understandings.

73. Those who understand their innate sinfulness and fallenness relative to God are capable of greater and deeper humility than those who believe that they are innately good, and have serene confidence in the rightness of their feelings and opinions in areas unverifiable by science.

The Consequences of Opposing World Views

The failure of the "Enlightenment"

It was the belief of the so-called Enlightenment that we would be able to make a better world by rejecting religion and tradition and relying on reason alone. This dazzling vision of self-reform and self-improvement by a humanity emancipated from God has proven to be a mirage, a delusion, a failure. The twentieth century, which – according to the dreams of secularists – should have been the most enlightened, progressive, and civilized period in history, turned out to be vicious, brutal, and bloody. Even in societies that escaped the devastations of war and totalitarianism, the humanist dreams of peace and material prosperity have proven to be deeply dissatisfying.

Not only have the advances of science failed to bring peace, but the blessings of modern technology have given us more power than we know how to handle wisely. They have exponentially increased the destructiveness of the forces of evil without providing any compensatory moral safeguards. Indeed, what traditional moral safeguards did exist were systematically and proudly dismantled – and the result is what we are seeing today. We can reasonably expect that things will only get worse as those who deny God follow their own appetites and dreams into the modern and postmodern darkness and confusion.

Is there something wrong with human nature? Can it be that deep down we are not really so good after all? The Bible teaches that we are not basically good at all. It presents us mortals as, in and of ourselves, blind, foolish and lost. The Bible presents the world as a dark place. We read in I John that the whole world lies in wickedness. John also refers in the opening verses of his Gospel to Christ's light shining in the darkness of the world. Peter refers in his letters to the corruptions and pollutions of the world, and to the filthy conversations of the wicked. Paul describes the sinfulness of mankind well in his letter to the Romans, particularly in the long list of vices in the first chapter. In the third chapter of Romans he refers to those who are "Swift to shed blood" and says "Destruction and misery are in their ways." Their mouths are full of lies and poison and "The way of peace they have not known." Whoever says that the Bible presents a shallow and optimistic view of life should stop speaking of things they know nothing about.

These and other biblical teachings about the spiritual truths that govern the world and the reality of evil in the human soul are infinitely more relevant to an understanding of our world than are totally unsubstantiated, ridiculous, pseudo-scientific speculations about imaginary multiverses, or about a minute speck a micro-fraction of a centimeter in diameter that somehow exploded into an orderly cosmos governed by detailed and highly specific laws.[1] The Bible has much to say about important aspects of our existence that eternally transcend the exceedingly limited reach of the physical sciences and the clumsy groping of autonomous human reason.

The beneficial results of the Protestant Reformation

In his book *Civilization: The Six Killer Apps of Western Power*, historian Niall Ferguson comments in various places on the positive effects of the Protestant Reformation. For example, he credits the rise of modern Western civilization to both the Renaissance and the Reformation.[2] This should be a commonplace, but unfortunately it isn't. Ferguson also states that Luther's religious revolution preceded and "unintentionally begat" the intellectual revolution which followed. "Because of the central importance in Luther's thought of individual reading of the Bible, Protestantism encouraged literacy, not to mention printing, and these two things unquestionably encouraged economic development (the accumulation of human capital) as well as scientific study."[3]

As an example, Ferguson also refers to higher literacy rates brought to other parts of the world by Protestant missionaries. This was not merely cultural imperialism either. I once asked an educated African if he would like his country to return to the culture it had before the Westerners came – he laughed. Lamin Sanneh, a Gambian theologian, has some worthwhile comments on the importance of literacy often brought first by missionaries who devised writing systems, grammars, and dictionaries for previously illiterate peoples, and who did not just impose Western values but brought many benefits.[4] They taught people to read and write with no guarantee that this knowledge would be used only to teach Christianity.

Even those who attempt to link Luther's anti-Judaism to later disastrous developments in German history can still see his larger significance. Rubenstein and Roth, while strongly condemning Luther's attitudes toward the Jews, have this to say: "Luther did as much to discover the new world of the spirit as Columbus did to discover the territorial New World. If, as many historians and sociologists of religion maintain, the modern world is in large measure an unintended consequence of religious and cultural forces arising out of the Protestant Reformation, Luther can be seen as one of its seminal creators."[5] The revolutionary idea that people could approach the deepest questions of life on an individual basis, apart from outdated medieval Church dogmas and unthinking obedience to Church leaders, "personalized faith . . . Protestant faith emerged with the breakdown of the old medieval order and hastened the new social order."[6]

Historian Robert Wistrich, while severely criticizing Luther, also recognized the importance of Luther's "devastating assault on the corruption, falsehoods, and superstitions abounding in the papal Rome of his day."[7] It has been said that the Reformation sundered Europe's spiritual unity, but who needs a false and artificially imposed unity of so-called faith that has to be enforced by Inquisitions, torture, and murder? We are told that the Reformation led to many religious wars – but what do people think Europe was before the Reformation? Have they read any history at all? Why does it need to be explained that there were countless wars in Europe for two thousand years and more before the Reformation. The Thirty Years War – constantly presented as an example of religious strife – was indeed sparked by religion, but quickly became an old-fashioned dynastic power struggle with Catholics aiding Protestants against their Catholic rivals.

One historian wrote of the violence that afflicted Europe before religious conflicts were mitigated by secularism. Is that why the twentieth century was the most peaceful century the world has ever known, because of the blessings of secularism? Consideration of these subjects is vastly complicated by those whose devotion to their materialist ideology makes it difficult for them to discuss religion objectively. Is it rational to blame Christianity for poison gas, napalm, and all of the other weapons of modern destruction? It was not Christian teaching that transformed war from a limited affair of the battlefield to something vastly greater, more vicious and destructive. Is it not in fact ridiculous for people who flatter themselves on their objectivity to give science credit for all of the advances of modern technology, yet exempt science from any blame for its abuses?

Another historian spoke of the Reformation and Counter-Reformation eras as a terrible period in which people and books were burned "regularly" – but Solzhenitsyn wrote in his *Gulag Archipelago* of the vast numbers of books and manuscripts destroyed by the KGB. The Nazis too burned books, all of this in the twentieth century. It is true of course that the Reformation was a time of deep religious conflict, but at the spiritual center of that conflict was the vital and necessary question of liberty. Are we to be in spiritual subjection to an authoritarian church-state structure which tells us what to believe and demands unthinking and unquestioning obedience? Or are we to seek out our own understanding and believe as seems right to us? This was at the heart of the Reformation – and docile obedience to Rome in the sixteenth century would not have ushered in a golden age of peace anyway. Conflict is endemic to human existence, and appears in every age, every civilization. This is due to human sin and disobedience to God.

We need spiritual liberty, and the liberty brought by the Reformation to think and to believe freely was a very important reason why science and learning flourished in northern Europe as they did nowhere else in the world. John Montgomery has written an entire chapter on the relationship of science to Protestantism, and effectively refutes charges of Luther being hostile to science, or opposing Copernicus' theory.[8] There are no negative comments from Luther on the theory after 1543, when Copernicus *De revolutionibus* was first published, and Luther's friend Philip Melanchthon and other second generation reformers came to support Copernicus (as Montgomery also shows). They were deeply involved in the beginnings of the coming scientific revolution. Secularists like to talk about the persecution of Galileo – as a non-Catholic, I feel that has nothing to do with me, and nothing to do with Christ or the New Testament. Also, many people, not only Luther and not only Christians, but also dedicated Aristotelians, found the new idea of the solar system hard to accept at first.

Neither was Luther hostile to the life of the mind. When he said that Madame Reason was the devil's whore, he was not speaking of the power of reason by which we learn languages, analyze a logical problem, design a building, or seek a cure for illness. He was speaking of reason in opposition to God, and the many ways it seeks to escape from God. Luther was a deeply learned man with a thorough grasp of the philosophical and theological controversies of his day, and was not in any sense the coarse buffoon or comic strip character some have tried to make him out to be. His best works have a deep spiritual power conspicuously absent from too many Evangelical authors today.

Much has also been said about the Protestant work ethic, without appreciating that it is general Christian teachings of the purpose of life, accountability to God, the need to be sober, diligent, kind to others, obey the laws, be faithful to one's spouse, avoid drunkenness and crime, and to treat others as you would like to be treated that contributed greatly to the political, scientific, and economic advance of the West. Even a noted secularist like the biologist Jacques Monod recognized that the emergence of modern science only in the "Christian West" and nowhere else might be attributable to some extent to the character of the Christian religion.[9] And, while basic Christian truths are neither Catholic nor Protestant but biblical, it was Luther and the Reformers who made these truths more accessible to many people in a real and living way, apart from the dead hand of superstition, relics, saints, and endless burdensome regulations.

In this context Ferguson quotes a Chinese scholar's recognition of Christianity's foundational importance to Western culture: ". . . we have realized that the heart of your culture is your religion: Christianity. That is why the West has been so powerful. The Christian moral foundation of social and cultural life was what made possible the emergence of capitalism and then the successful transition to democratic politics. We don't have any doubt about this." Ferguson quotes another Chinese academic to the effect that —such concepts as freedom, human rights, tolerance, equality, justice, democracy, the rule of law," and other positive aspects of Western civilization were incomprehensible without the "Christian understanding of transcendence."[10]

For much of Europe, the modern understanding of these qualities was developed according to Protestant concepts of freedom of thought but within the immeasurably vast metaphysical framework of biblical truth. That life has a higher purpose; that there are objective standards of right and wrong; that we will be held accountable in the next life for how we lived in this one; that there is a personal God and that love, rationality, and humanity are not merely unexplainable materialistic accidents but are related to the origins of the cosmos in God – these and other related concepts enlarge and enrich the soul, and add new dimensions to life. They are "truths of infinite moment . . . the highest themes which can challenge an immortal mind."[11]

This contrasts vividly with the emptiness and pointlessness of modern materialism, a poisonous soul-deadening fog that stifles the human spirit and warps our highest aspirations. No wonder modern art, literature, and music are so ugly and inferior. No wonder the modern age with its precious and vastly overrated scientific progress has produced marvels of death, destruction, and inhumanity unknown in the entire previous history of the world. Progress – but in which direction?

D.M. Lloyd-Jones wrote that "the Protestant Reformation liberated men and taught them to think for themselves."[12] This is not to say that the Protestants were always the good guys. Nor is it to deny the many problems and evils of Western society. Unlike the fantasy of Marxism based on its imaginary historical analysis, the Bible does not offer the delusion of a secular paradise on earth. It recognizes that there will be sin and evil until Christ returns, but it gives a higher moral standard, a hope, and a purpose that significantly impacted Western civilization for the good. Luther had a great deal to do with this.

It is no coincidence that the Jews were well (if not perfectly) treated in every single country that emerged out the Reformation. Even in Germany before the catastrophe of the First World War, the Jews had established deep roots and made great social and cultural progress. This was true to such an extent that many Jews were proud of their German cultural heritage. A Reform Jewish prayer book published in Germany in 1818 even went so far as to remove all prayers for a return to Israel, and for the Messiah to come. "They were fully content as Germans and could fulfill all their national aspirations as Germans in Germany,"[13] and had no further need of Israel or of a Messiah.

Francis Schaeffer writes, "For a long time Reformation ideas formed the basis of North European culture, and this extended to include that of the United States and English-speaking Canada, etc."[14] This does not mean that those countries were free from common human evils, or that all of the people in them were devout, Bible-believing Christians. It does mean that deeply influential concepts of God, his laws, and the afterlife provided a framework within which individual liberty could flourish along with respect for law. Because of the Bible, there was a sane balance between the social obligations and the political rights of the individual.

The worst excesses of secular anti-Jewish ideology that emerged in Germany in the nineteenth century and were foundational to Naziism came not out of the Reformation, but out of the widespread repudiation of Christianity that characterized a significant part of European culture in the beginnings of the modern era. They are more related to Hegel, Fichte, Schopenhauer, Nietzsche, Wagner and Haeckel, and even to Kant, than they are to the Reformation. When Hitler wrote in *Mein Kampf* that the Jews had no concept of an afterlife and were nothing but materialists,[15] he was elaborating on a theme introduced by Kant, not by Luther. 19th-century French secularism and socialism also had profoundly antisemitic elements, which were nourished and cherished by people who did not care about Luther or believe in the Bible. Their hatred of Judaism was due to the fact that its most fundamental teachings denied their delusional faith in human reason and progress.[16]

Remarkably, noted historian Robert Conquest devotes a chapter of one of his books to explaining how democracy became established in the West without even recognizing Christianity as an integral part of that. He sees religious truth as being related to fanaticism, irrationality, and the excesses of modern secular ideologies, and claims they all spring from the same root of irrationality. He equates the Bible and Marxist dogma as sacred texts to be followed by people in need of absolute truths and final answers. He equates 17th-century English religious extremists and Byzantine mobs fighting about religious issues with Nazis and Communists.[17]

What Conquest and others who share his now common views fail to recognize is that there are infinite and eternal differences between the Absolute Truth of God revealed in Jesus Christ and the Bible on the one hand, and the "Absolute Truths" of modern secularism as revealed to Marx, Lenin, Hitler, Darwin, Stalin and Mao on the other. In placing all sure conviction of truth – except for his own – under the same condemnation, Conquest fails to differentiate between "Do unto others as you would have them do unto you," as well as "We are liberated from God's law and can create our own paradise here in this life without him."

The Christian idea of Truth is very far from contradictory secular concepts that bubbled up out of the quagmires of modern secularism and denial of God. That we have immortal souls and are only being tested here for a short time on earth before standing to before God to be judged is a very powerful motive for the elevation of the individual personality above the demands of the state and of society. The loss of the sense of the divine origin and eternal destiny of the human soul is one of the main starting points for fascism, which in the end inevitably subordinates the individual to the group (since there is nothing higher than the group, personified by the state).

Alcide de Gasperi (a victim of Mussolini, and later leader of Italy's first postwar government in 1945) rightly said: "The theoretical and practical principles of fascism are the antithesis of the Christian concept of the state, which lays down that the natural rights of personality, family, and society exist before the state."[18] Or, as Nicolai Berdyaev put it: ". . . the Christian ethic is more individual than social; for the human soul is worth more than all the kingdoms of this world."[19] Human worth as derived from God was an essential concept in the development of Western society. Its disappearance contributed directly to the threats to democracy and the losses of liberty and prosperity we are now experiencing in the 3rd decade of the 21st century.

This is hard (if not impossible) for many limited modern thinkers to grasp, especially when they have come to think of the religious impulse in and of itself as false, irrational, harmful and potentially dangerous. When a highly praised historian writes that the vicious and brutal secular mass murderer and tyrant Lenin had a zeal for humanity comparable to some Christian saints, we realize how remote much of our modern intelligentsia is from a fair understanding of Christianity. Since when does the "love of saints" have anything to do with Lenin's dictatorship, his secret police, his executions? To say that Lenin was animated by the same spirit and zeal which motivated Luther, Calvin and many others an amazing statement by someone who obviously has no understanding of Christ's teachings. Neither does he have any understanding of the many Christians who have followed those teachings imperfectly, but at least well enough to live common, peaceful and ordinary lives far below the exalted vision of ivory tower historians.

Paul Johnson recognizes that Lenin's methods "corresponded in a curious way to the Marxist perception of the world."[20] Curious, that an avowed Marxist should look at things in a Marxist way, even though he adapted Marx's theories to a foreign context. A true man of God, according to the Bible's standards, does not aim to bring about paradise on earth. Unlike Marx, Lenin, Stalin, Pol Pot, Castro and Mao, the leaders and followers of the Reformation did not think that human reason was a sufficient guide, or that dictatorship of the favored group would bring peace on earth (after all of the enemies of human happiness had been crushed like "insects," to use one of Lenin's terms).

Bible-believing Christians know that full happiness cannot be obtained in this life due to the sinfulness of human nature, and so we look for the final resolution of all injustice in the next life, in the world to come. Only the most fanatical secularists with their man-centered, self-centered world views are vain enough to believe that they can reshape humanity according to their theoretical blueprints, and that their opponents can be slaughtered in the millions without a qualm for the sake of an imaginary future happiness.

Linking Lenin to Christians rather than to Marx's hateful intolerance shows – in my view – a sad disorientation. Both Marx and Lenin were fanatical and intolerant atheists. Both had a burning zeal to destroy the status quo, and build their fantasy world on the ashes. Both had contempt for those who contradicted them; were separated from reality and ignorant of human nature and real-world economics; and relied on dictatorship to impose their solutions (which they knew would never be accepted otherwise). Marx's famed dictatorship of the proletariat was not just a theory. He rightly understood that religion, capitalism and private property would never be eliminated without it.

Both Marx and Lenin had contempt for democracy, and both made the ludicrous claim that their nonsensical theories were scientific. Finally – and this shows their deep spiritual kinship with Hitler – both thought they were the saviors of mankind, and those who disagreed with them were enemies to be destroyed. Yes, they had differences, and Lenin adapted Marx to a different situation, but in spirit Lenin, Marx, and Hitler all thought they could remake the world according to their liking, in defiance of God and his laws. Their deluded theories – all of them predicated upon a rejection of the Bible – brought misery and ruin to countless millions.

Can some people really not see the difference between adherence to the truth of Christ, and adherence to the useless fantasy of a paradise established after private property and religion have been abolished by the dictatorship [!?] of the proletariat? No, they can't see the difference. To them, Christ's heavenly kingdom as exemplified by the Sermon on the Mount is comparable to the earthly kingdom of secular fanatics who want to exterminate or enslave the worthless wretches that dare to oppose the future happiness of mankind as dreamed of by them in their infallible wisdom. It is with good reason that Thomas Oden contrasted modern arrogance with Christianity's sane and realistic preference for "modest, incremental shifts toward proximate justice" instead of "totally revolutionary redefinitions of the universal human order. This requires a scaling down of social planning and a scaling up of personal accountability."[21]

Biblical Christianity as revived by the Reformation (however imperfectly) was foundational to Western democracy, individual liberty, and the subordination of the state to a higher law. It also helped to restrain (if not to eliminate) sin, which is why in our post-biblical age we are now having an explosion of such sins as crime, drugs, pornography, abortion and general immorality in its various forms – and, not coincidentally, a huge increase in the power of government with a corresponding loss of individual rights. There's no need to mention the Crusades or the Inquisition here either. They had nothing to do with the teachings of Christ, and have nothing to do with the vast majority of Christians who have ever lived.

John Calvin

Some people try to bring Calvin into their condemnations of religious fanaticism. They have even compared him to modern totalitarians – as if Calvin's Geneva had had concentration camps and secret police; as if Calvin had slaughtered, starved and enslaved millions; as if people were not free to leave Geneva at any time and go to another city in the same country (without having to worry about passports or visas, needless to say).

Is it even possible to reason with someone who compares 16th-century Geneva to the Soviet Union or to Nazi Germany? The callous mass-murderer Lenin, seeking Marx's mirage of an earthly paradise, butchered more people in a single day with his infamous "merciless mass terror" than were killed in Geneva in a century – and Genevan practices of capital punishment were the norm in Europe at that time. Lenin's practices were not the norm. Suffice it to say that the very great influence on England and America of biblical Protestantism in general, and Calvinism in particular, did not lead to the savage and fanatical atheistic and secular excesses of conceited moderns who thought that their own paltry intelligences were sufficient to work out the future happiness of mankind and remake the world without God.

Neither do Catholic and Protestant disputes about the eucharist in the 16th century or disputes about the Trinity in earlier centuries have anything to do with the problem of modern totalitarianism, or with the belief that it is legitimate to exterminate large numbers of people for the sake of a future imaginary happiness of mankind. Attempts to connect "warring theologians" to Communism or National Socialism completely omit the fact that no "warring theologians" ever put into practice the horrors of the Soviet Union or the Third Reich. These sorts of comparisons are very wide of the mark and are motivated solely by blind and unthinking hostility to religion, not by reason, logic, or objective consideration of factual evidence, or even elementary honesty. Some historians seem to think that attacking religious beliefs that they do not understand is part of their professional calling.

It took denial of the immortality of the individual human soul to legitimize modern mass murders for the imagined good of mankind. The Huns, the Vikings and the Mongols enjoyed killing, but they weren't clever enough and educated enough to use philosophy to justify their bloodlust as a positive good, morally justifiable and beneficial. We must give modernity credit for modern crimes – unless, of course, our purpose is only to express our dislike for Christianity at every opportunity, whether appropriate or not. Likening Lenin to a religious fanatic is the kind of unhistorical bias which completely fails to comprehend that Christianity never in its many centuries of history produced someone like Lenin with a totalitarian state at his command.

A brief overview of liberal German Protestantism

Many students of German history have little or no sympathy for or understanding of religion, and so have no idea how much the churches had been weakened in the 19th century by the advances of liberal Protestantism. Such a progression did not happen overnight, but had a long history.

As early as the 1670s, some German Christians were concerned that Lutheranism had stagnated, that it had become merely a matter of ecclesiastical authority and intellectual discussions of doctrine without life, power, light, or genuine spiritual experience. This led to the emergence of Pietism, an attempt to find a more authentic experience within the Lutheran Protestant tradition.[22]

Along with a dull, lifeless orthodoxy and individual attempts to find a more authentic experience, a third strand of Protestantism emerged in the nineteenth century. This is generally called theological liberalism, and developed out of the attempts of many Christian leaders to compromise biblical teachings with what they took to be the equally important or even more important insights derived from secular philosophy and from science. It is too little understood by many that long before 1933 much of modern German Protestantism had gone so far from the teachings of Luther as to have become a different religion entirely.

In his book *Reasonable Faith*, William Lane Craig presents a brief but effective overview of the internal spiritual collapse of the German churches. He states "The flood of Deist thought and literature that poured into eighteenth-century Germany from England and France wrought a crisis in German orthodox theology."[23] No longer capable of defending biblical doctrines now judged contrary to reason, but unwilling to dispense with Christianity altogether, increasingly Christian leaders were willing to concede that the Bible was full of mistakes, errors, myths, and false teachings, but somehow contained some spiritual and ethical truths nevertheless. Such views quickly became dominant among official German Protestantism.

Significantly, Bismarck's *Kulturkampf* ("culture struggle"), the attempt to break the power of the Catholic Church in Germany, was not based on Lutheran biblical interpretations of salvation, church authority, and the Bible. It was because Catholic opposition to modern trends made the Roman Church into "the enemy of liberalism, of belief in reform, above all of opposition to the cultivation of the human intellect and spirit in civic society"[24] through modern education emphasizing science and the humanities. Also, after the assertion of papal infallibility by a Vatican Council in 1870, loyalty to the Pope was seen as incompatible with loyalty to the Kaiser and the newly formed German Empire. Protestantism, on the other hand, was seen as more amenable to progress because of its abandonment of traditional doctrines.

Nineteenth-century Germany, far from being a Christian country based on the Reformation, was known throughout the Christian world as the leading source of new ideas of biblical criticism that denied the divine authority and truth of the Bible. Church historian Philip Schaff wrote in the nineteenth century that the "critical and historical rationalism which was born and matured in this century in the land of Luther" was based on "opposition to the supernatural and the miraculous."[25] Francis Schaeffer states, "But how did theological liberalism come about? In order to understand this, we must go back about 250 years to Germany where theological liberalism was born."[26]

The same writer also says in this context that already by the middle of the eighteenth century German universities had lost a living and vital Lutheran orthodoxy, and notes "In church history a cycle seems to recur: living orthodoxy moves to dead orthodoxy and then to heterodoxy."[27] This is not to deny that some genuine Christian influence remained – but Christianity was no longer intellectually dominant. The forces of theological conservatism fought a futile rearguard action, but powerful forces of change made the old-time religion seem less and less relevant to many. Those who did not abandon it altogether thought they could adapt Christianity to the new times. This would, it was hoped, make Christianity more acceptable to sophisticated modern man, but in the end this spirit of surrender and compromise contributed in no small measure to the pathetic collapse of the German churches in the 20th century.

So-called higher biblical criticism – inappropriately called a "science" – was based on the principle that the Bible was to be treated as an ordinary book, written by ordinary means, and hence vulnerable to distortions and errors. Theology became merely humanistic interpretations and explanations of what were once considered to be eternal foundations, and the Bible came to be studied as a cultural product of the times in which it was written. A "profound ideological and philosophical shift was taking place," and liberal theology "tended simply to follow the curve of secular naturalism."[28] It was not because of Luther that German "Protestant" "theologians" followed Hitler. They had been abandoning Reformation principles and following the world for a century and more before Hitler came to power.

This theological progressivism included among others the ideas that Jesus did not die on the cross, but only swooned and later revived; that the Jews had no divine revelation but invented a fictionalized history; that the Gospels were not accurate records of what Christ did and taught; that the most important thing was to be sincere (surely that would be good enough for a God of love); that the apostles did not receive their teaching from Christ but made things up as it seemed right to them. All of this, of course, used words such as "Christ . . . faith . . . the Gospel . . . love . . . salvation . . . grace" in a manner very confusing to those who are ignorant of these issues and judge only by outward appearances. This has been aptly summarized by J. Gresham Machen, who wrote that modern theological liberalism is "a totally diverse type of religious belief, which is only the more destructive of the Christian faith because it makes use of traditional Christian terminology."[29]

People who like to imagine that Germany was a Christian country, "the most Christian country on earth," either know little about the subject, or else do not have the faintest idea of what Christianity is. They have almost certainly never heard of the eighteenth-century professor Herrmann Samuel Reimarus. This individual wrote a lengthy critique of Christianity, published after his death by the famed humanist Gottfried Lessing. This Deistic work denied the resurrection of Christ, the biblical miracles, and the Old Testament narratives. Reimarus claimed that Jesus failed in his earthly mission and was executed, after which the disciples stole his body and fabricated a story about a resurrection.

In the first half of the nineteenth century David Friedrich Strauss wrote a book, *The Life of Jesus* (*Leben Jesu*) (1835). He did not want to dismiss Christianity outright as a mere apostolic fraud like Reimarus did, so he invented the theory that the myths and legends of Christianity developed slowly and naturally over time. The resurrection of Christ never occurred, but it did have spiritual significance – as other myths also contained deeper meanings. Again according to

Craig, "Strauss's work completely altered the tone and course of German theology."[30]

Modern German "theologians" did not have to worry about the mistakes, errors, contradictions, and seemingly unscientific parts of the Bible. They could concede all of that, and still speak about the Bible's religious and spiritual significance – but unfortunately, with the Christ of faith detached from the Christ of history, theology entered a never-never land of speculation grounded solidly on thin air. This led to a sort of imaginary faith in some idea of an unknown Christ without the certainty of a literal, factual, historical Bible, the new, secular faith that we find in Bultmann, Barth, Bonhoeffer and other popular modern theologians.

According to Francis Schaeffer, "Karl Barth's basic position was this: Of course, the Bible has all kinds of mistakes in it, but it doesn't matter; believe it religiously." Bultmann was far more extreme than Barth, and openly described fundamental biblical doctrines as mythology. With this neo-orthodoxy, to quote Schaeffer again, "theology stepped from the solid earth of rationality into a land where anything can happen."[31] As the nineteenth century progressed, liberal and neo-orthodox so-called theology not surprisingly turned out to be helpless before newer and more powerful ideas such as Hegelianism, Romanticism, Marxism, Darwinism, social Darwinism, Freudianism, and National Socialism.

Reimarus and Strauss were not isolated figures. They represented deep and broad trends. Traditional biblical Christianity became increasingly out of date, and more and more people looked not to philosophy but to science and theology. In the words of Alister McGrath, "As clerical power began to decline in the eighteenth century, Western society began to look to others for moral vision and intellectual inspiration. It found such leaders in the growing community of intellectuals."[32] Too many people talk about

"Christian Europe" and "Christian Germany" as if the great movement toward secularism that began in the eighteenth century and became increasingly dominant in the 19th century had never occurred. McGrath continues,

> At some point, perhaps one that can never be determined with historical accuracy, Western society came to believe that it should look elsewhere than to its clergy for guidance. Instead, they turned to the intellectuals, who were able to portray their clerical opponents as lazy fools who could do no more than unthinkingly repeat the slogans and nostrums of an increasingly distant past. A new future lay ahead, and society needed brave new thinkers to lead them to its lush Promethean pastures.[33]

It is difficult to overemphasize the profoundly irreligious nature of the upper reaches of German intellectual society, though of course much traditional belief still remained elsewhere. Hegel, Kant, Feuerbach, Schopenhauer and other leading lights of German philosophy were none of them believers in the truth of the Bible or of the necessity of faith in Christ for salvation of sin. Kant and Hegel have been called "Protestant" philosophers not because of their ideas, which were thoroughly unbiblical. They have been mistaken for Protestants because they were born and lived in a certain longitude and latitude; grew up in a vaguely Protestant milieu; stressed the beneficial effects of Protestant Christianity in Europe's cultural development; or had a great influence on later liberal Protestants who found human philosophy more inspiring than divine revelation – but no serious student of philosophy has ever claimed those men were devout Christians who believed that Jesus died on the cross so that they might be saved from their sins and escape God's justice on the day of judgment as the divinely inspired Bible taught.

When someone claims that Kant reaffirmed the Christian worldview in his philosophy, we may reasonably infer that he has no knowledge of Christianity, or of Kantian philosophy, or both. In a well-known essay *An Answer to the Question: What is Enlightenment?* Kant expressed deep hostility to unchanging divinely revealed dogmas as representing the immaturity of mankind. He saw eternal unchanging truths as fetters that hindered the free spiritual and intellectual progress of mankind. In *Religion Within the Limits of Reason Alone* Kant revealed his open disbelief in many basic Christian doctrines. The title itself is a denial of divine revelation as a source of knowledge. Because of the cultural constraints of that day Kant was compelled to say some nice things about religion from time to time, but at the heart of his philosophy is a rejection of the traditional concept of a personal God, and an affirmation of the power of autonomous human reason.[34]

There has never been a Christian country

Jesus said, "strait is the gate, and narrow is the way, which leadeth unto life, and few there be that find it." In that same context he also taught, " wide is the gate, and broad is the way, that leadeth to destruction, and many there be which go in thereat." This says that a great many people will be lost, and few will be saved. Even allowing for greater concentrations of Christians in this or that period, has anyone ever seriously maintained that the majority of Americans, in any period of our history, were faithful and obedient followers of Christ, dying to self, taking up the cross, and walking in the straight and narrow way of biblical holiness?

Moreover, we read in I John that "we know that we are of God, and the whole world lieth in wickedness." The whole world lies in wickedness – surely that must include the United States. No serious believer in the truths of Scripture has ever said that this did not apply to some particular exceptional country – and when we consider the facts of American history, do we not see ample instances of the various sins that have afflicted every other part of the globe since the dawn of recorded history? Admittedly, at its best, America has offered a degree of liberty and prosperity unknown to much of the human race throughout much of history, but even there we can see great spiritual darkness.

Evil does not merely consist of flagrant and outward sins such as hatred, murder, sexual immorality, and so on. There is also an evil that is nothing more than polite indifference to God; the belief that we can manage our own lives; that we have no need to even acknowledge, let alone obey, our Creator. There are many Americans who are friendly and outwardly harmless people, but their ignorance of God is spiritual darkness, and the breeding ground for many more blatant and obvious sins – the same sort of sins that have been and can be found in every other part of the world.

Is anyone so foolish to imagine that Africa and North America were paradises of social harmony and justice before the Europeans arrived? The problem is sin and evil in the human heart. The worst sins of the Europeans in America have been equaled and even surpassed in other parts of the globe. Have any of those who are so obsessed with hatred of America today ever read about China, or modern Europe, or the failed states of modern Africa, and considered the massacres, famines, oppression, and hatreds that have occurred there? Some of the people today who are making the most noise about "justice" today are themselves afflicted by the very same sinful passions that they condemn in others.

But getting back to the founding of America, was it ever really a Christian country? Did any of the founding fathers actually believe in the Bible? The Declaration of Independence mentions "Life, liberty, and the pursuit of happiness" – but nothing about our obligations to believe in God and follow his laws. That is a purely secular document, with nothing of Christ about it. The founders set up an excellent system, humanly speaking, and we can be grateful for that as part of God's providence for us, but that system now seems to be going the way of all other systems.

Jesus Christ did not come to earth to set up a political system. Neither did he advocate rebellion against Rome because the Jews did not have parliamentary representation in the Roman government, and were subject to taxation without representation. Jesus was more concerned with where people will spend eternity. What does it profit us, if we live in a free and independent country but are lost and die and spend eternity in hell? What does it harm us, if we live under a benevolent colonial system like that of George the Third (a system far less onerous and burdensome when it comes to taxation than the system we now live under) yet die and go to heaven?

Christianity has been accused of being too otherworldly, of focusing on the next life to the exclusion of this one, and it is true that we should not neglect our duties in this life. However, it is better, as Christ taught, to live in poverty and misery and die and go to heaven, than to have prosperity and liberty and die and go to hell.

And what about Romans chapter 13? Paul says that the God has ordained the authorities, and that those who rebel bring condemnation upon themselves. We note that Jesus and the apostles lived under a foreign conquering power that committed many what we would call today human rights violations, yet they did not advocate rebellion. Could it be that the entire American revolution was nothing but rebellion and sin against God? What if we had remained under British domination and gotten our independence gradually as Canada and Australia did? Would that have been so terrible? It would have prevented the entire Civil War, if British law had prevailed and slavery had been outlawed in the entire country by the Slavery Abolition Act of 1833.

Well, what's done is done. We have to serve Christ in the situation as we now find it – but exaggerated pictures of a formerly Christian America will not help us now. And what if America is doomed? What if the moral decay and corruption has proceeded so far that the country cannot be saved? What if we are going to be subjected to economic collapse, or to government tyranny and the complete loss of basic rights, or to social breakdown, or to all of these and yet more? What if we cannot save the system? How real will our spiritual blessings in Christ be to us then?

Germany prior to World War 2 was not a Christian country

Attempts to understand the terrible mystery of the Holocaust have sometimes or often been led astray by the misconception that Germany was historically a Christian country. That being so, it has been reasoned that Christianity must have had something to do with the emergence of Hitler and his crimes. But what if Germany was not a Christian country? And what if modern Germany in particular had long since rejected and abandoned earlier Christian influences?

Peter Watson's detailed survey of modern German culture, *The German Genius*, has little to say about traditional Christianity (except for a brief discussion of Pietism that emerged in the late seventeenth century). None of the greats of nineteenth-century German philosophy, science, music, or literature are presented as devout Christians. Watson did illustrate the decline of religious influence with some revealing statistics, though. He stated that the percentage of theological books published in Germany fell from 46 percent of the total in 1625 to a mere 6 percent in 1800.[35] He also spoke of Romantic concepts such as (among other things) that of the "outcast genius . . . rebelling against a tame and philistine society," or "martyrs, tragic heroes who fought for their beliefs against overwhelming odds."[36] These concepts were easily applied to Hitler by his admirers.

Peter Viereck's dated but still useful *Meta-politics: The Roots of the Nazi Mind* sees German romanticism as more significant to the emergence of Nazi ideas than any conventionally religious thinkers.

People who think Germany was a Christian country understand neither Christian teaching nor German intellectual and cultural history. Germany was not immune to the modernist revolution of the eighteenth and nineteenth centuries. This revolution included a massive turning away by much of Europe's intellectual elite from revealed, traditional religion. Watson writes that "With the Mass in B Minor and Bach's death, a whole artistic, spiritual, cultural, and intellectual world was at an end."[37] The influence and prestige of the churches had been steadily declining in Europe ever since the "Enlightenment," and the churches in Germany were deeply influenced by this trend.

This included, of course, the loss of traditional ethics which had been derived either from Christianity or from cultural adaptations of Christianity. New understandings of ethics and morality followed, based on speculative philosophy, on Darwinian science, on feeling and intuition – not on any supposed laws of God which we were all universally obligated to obey. The divine origin of the human soul was lost in the turbulent floods of modernism, to be replaced by – by what? By the beliefs that we were nothing but animals; that conventional morality was a hindrance to the full development of the personality; that we could do whatever seemed right in our own eyes with no regard to any higher authority, except perhaps for the state.

It should not be necessary to mention this, and is not necessary most of the time – only when people want to blame Christianity for modern sins. Some people seem to believe that there was a Protestant Reformation in 1517, then there was World War I and the Weimar era and Hitler came to power. Have these people heard of Nietzsche, of Wagner, Schopenhauer, Beethoven, Goethe, Kant, Fichte, Hegel and Schiller? Or, if they have at least heard of those names, do they believe that one of those key figures in modern German history believed that the Bible was the word of God? That there would be a resurrection from the dead, and we would stand before the judgment seat of Jesus Christ? The belief that this present, visible world is all we can know is one of the foundational blunders of modernism.

Goethe laughed at Christianity. He wrote a phenomenally successful book, *The Sorrows of Young Werther*, in which the protagonist fell deeply in love with a married woman – and what did Werther do? Discover while reading the Bible that his passion was sinful, and so repent and seek forgiveness for his illicit lusts? No, he killed himself. Beethoven's Ninth Symphony does not represent Christian values. It is a celebration of mankind on the mountaintop, glorying in his power. Beethoven used Schiller's lyrics in the choral movement – "Joy! Spark of the gods! Daughter of Elysium! Drunk with fire, we approach your holiness! Your magic binds mankind together!" What does these foolish and empty words have to do with the teachings of Christ?

The "Enlightenment" of Kant and many others, that denied revelation and relied on autonomous human reason; Romanticism, with its emphasis on feeling and intuition, and its rejection of conventional morality; the idealistic philosophy of Hegel, which presented a higher spiritual reality totally different from that of orthodox Christianity, one discovered by reason alone and only a figment of human imagination; Fichte, who made the nation into a substitute god, the source of our meaning and purpose; the emphasis on the classics and the Greek revival, which taught that the Jews were barbarians, while "only the Greeks and Romans possessed a higher *Geisteskultur* (intellectual culture)," and that only the Greek and Roman civilizations were "the source and basis of culture"[38] – an understanding of these things is not necessary if one's sole purpose is to attack Christianity in an ignorant and badly educated way.

In a treatise entitled "On Classical Studies," Hegel authoritatively decreed from his philosophical perch on high in his study that "Greek literature in the first place, Roman in the second" were the true foundations of higher learning. He further exclaimed in secular humanist rapture that "The perfection and glory of those masterpieces" would provide a "spiritual bath" and a "secular baptism that first and indelibly attunes and tinctures the soul." The world of Greece and Rome was "the fairest that has ever been . . . The works of the ancients contain the most noble food in the most noble form."[39] In the school where Nietzsche studied as a teenager "the students breathed the air not of modern Europe but of ancient Greece and Rome and of the Germany of Goethe and Schiller."[40]

We should not forget Social Darwinism, the belief that Darwin's theory should be applied to people in a new ethic of life in which mercy and compassion had no reality and no place. There were also Marxism; Freudianism; empiricism; materialism; pantheism; extreme nationalism, that often included the German nation and race as agents of a Hegelian World Spirit; modern movements in art, literature and music; the racist, antisemitic and militaristic Folkish movement from which National Socialism directly emerged – and all of them assumed and were predicated upon the irrelevance of the Bible. It is not in Christianity, but in rebellion against Christianity, that we must seek an understanding of the origins of National Socialist ideology.

Even in the first half of the nineteenth century, the German-Jewish poet Heinrich Heine saw the dangers inherent in the new ideas that emerged subsequent to the "Enlightenment's" declaration of independence from God. Heine foresaw that "Kantian criticism, Fichtean transcendental idealism, and even *Naturphilosophie* [nature philosophy]," with their repudiation of traditional ethics and values, were extremely dangerous. "Because of these very doctrines," he elaborated, "revolutionary forces have developed which are simply biding their time to break out and to be able to fill the world with horror and admiration." Heine predicted that people armed with these new ideas "will mercilessly tear up the soil of our European life in order to destroy the past to its very roots. Armed Fichteans will come onto the scene, who, with fanatic will, will be untamable by self-interest or fear." They will be "inflexible in a social upheaval" and "not moved by any traditional reverence."[41]

People wonder how the Nazis could have emerged out of German culture. It is too little considered that German culture was part of the problem, and in fact provided fertile soil for ideas that were later to prove integral and foundational to National Socialism. Watson goes so far as to state that even as early as the first half of the nineteenth century "neohumanist *Bildung*," a secular search for inner fulfillment by education, without depending on religion, was "the cultural philosophy of the Prussian state."[42] There was a common belief "that spiritual emancipation through education in the humanities was the true path to (inner) freedom." The belief in submission to divine authority as expressed in the Bible and interpreted by the church was a rapidly fading memory. Those who think that the leading lights of German philosophy, history, art, music, literature, and science were inspired by belief in the Bible, or that Prussian domination of Germany was the result of Bismarck's faithful adherence to the teachings of Jesus Christ only reveal their complete ignorance of this subject. That Christianity should be rejected as false and out of date, and then be blamed when things later go wrong, is more than a little ridiculous. Some people are incapable of admitting that the modernist experiment was, in the case of Germany, a disastrous failure.

Gordon Craig's in-depth history of Germany from 1866 to the end of World War II contains ample evidence of the secularization of German society. An overview of the educational system emphasizes the humanistic content, especially in the classics and the natural sciences. Philosophical trends in German universities did not reflect Christian values. The increasing importance of the behavioral and social "sciences," Darwin, Comte, materialism and mechanism, neo-Kantianism, the study of German history and literature as "a handmaid for the salvation of the nation"[43]– it would be possible I believe to write a detailed book about German universities in the second half of the nineteenth century without even using the name of Jesus once. No doubt such books have been written.

The history of Germany just cited shows that even before 1900 Germans themselves were concerned about the increasingly evident signs of moral decline and decay. Incidents of rape doubled in Berlin during the six years of 1872-1878, along with a significant increase in crime in general. Prostitution and public drunkenness increased, along with "a relaxation in public morals" and a "massive preoccupation with sex" in the theater as seen in "the crudest kind of bedroom farces."[44]

When it comes to the Weimar Republic, the premature experiment in democracy that was terminated by Hitler in 1933, its secular nature should not need to be even mentioned. The chapter title in Watson's cultural history of Germany reads "Weimar: The Golden Age of Twentieth-Century Physics, Philosophy, and History."[45] This chapter and the one preceding deal with Niels Bohr, Werner Heisenberg, breakthroughs in modern cinema, Expressionist painting, Walter Gropius and the Bauhaus, Marx and Freud, Herbert Marcuse, the music of Schoenberg and the poetry of Brecht, Marlene Dietrich and *The Blue Angel* – I may have missed something, but I did not see one word about Jesus, the Bible, Heaven, Hell, a day of judgment or forgiveness of sins in the two chapters.

There was a consistent decline in the idea of God from the end of the eighteenth century to the end of the nineteenth. From the transcendent, truly divine God of the Scriptures to the theoretical, inactive and profoundly worthless God of Kant and the many other deists; to Hegel's nebulous and impersonal World Spirit; to Schopenhauer's blindly striving cosmic Will; to the vague philosophical Creator of the Darwinist Ernst Haeckel, the "Almighty," a vague cosmic something that worked according to scientific law and was understood by human reason alone (which was close if not identical to Hitler's conception); to the feverish pronouncement of the death of God by Nietzsche – the idea of God faded and finally died in the minds of many. The churches, Protestant and Catholic, had long since lost their dominant position and were incapable of significantly influencing the course of German history.

Intriguingly, these declining concepts of God have been summed up in a remarkable passage in Goethe's *Faust*. Suggesting that the well-known Bible verse "In the beginning was the Word" was inadequate, Goethe proposed replacing "Word" (traditional, revealed religion) with "Mind" (human wisdom, whether religious or secular). This didn't seem adequate, so he suggested replacing "Mind" with "Power." Finally he suggests "Deed," "In the beginning was the Deed."[46] From divine revelation to human wisdom, and thence to power and action unrestrained by any concept of divine law – this follows a spiritual law of descent just as real as any law of Newton's. Without God, we decline, and this descent ended, after many unpredictable windings and turnings, in National Socialism. This does not mean a general cultural awareness of God and earlier strong religious cultural influences were sufficient to create paradise on earth - they were not – but they did exercise some real and badly needed restraint. It took modern ideology based on human wisdom to set up the signposts and pave the way to Auschwitz.

These changes were accompanied by an increasing hostility to Christianity. Nietzsche is the most well-known example of this, but – while more extreme in his hatred than others (some might even say "fanatical" or "blindly irrational") – he was by no means alone. That traditional, orthodox Christianity was contrary to reason, as determined by philosophy; that it was contrary to science, and especially to the supposed truth of Darwinism; that Christianity was unGermanic, unhealthy, an alien Semitic import not suited to the warlike German spirit; that Christianity had originated in India but was later corrupted by Semitic influences; that Paul had distorted, falsified and Judaized the teachings of an Aryan Christ; that Christian ethics were contrary to the realities of life – these and other ideas were increasingly current in influential circles among the German intelligentsia long before 1933.

A closer look at German liberal Protestantism

German liberal theology had an enormous influence on the rest of European and American Protestantism in the 19th and early 20th centuries. Since their use of standard theological terminology in previously unknown ways has caused a great deal of confusion, both within the churches and without, a closer look at this phenomenon is warranted. This is not merely a question of German culture, but pertains to the West as a whole.

Long before 1900, a great number of seminaries and churches in Germany were staffed and pastored by people who did not believe in the Bible as the divinely inspired and inerrant word of God. They called themselves "Christians" and were so considered in the eyes of the world, but they had, in effect, invented a new religion which was essentially worldly philosophy in a religious disguise – and their views were often expressed in an evasive and misleading way so as not to upset common people who (they felt) were not sophisticated enough to understand. Kant suggested that pastors who accepted the new ideas but wanted to continue in their present occupation could have it both ways:

> In the same way [as a military officer may obey an order out of necessity while personally finding fault with it], a clergyman is bound to instruct his pupils and his

congregation in accordance with the doctrines of the church he serves, for he was employed by it on that condition. But as a scholar, he is completely free as well as obliged to impart to the public all his carefully considered, well- intentioned thoughts on the mistaken aspects of those doctrines ... there is nothing in this which need trouble the conscience.[47]

Apart from illustrating Kant's contempt for traditional religion and his ignorance of the nature of the church, this raises questions about his own grasp of ethical principles. For example, did he deny the right of a people to rebel against the government because he knew it would make the Prussian authorities happy, while at the same time he had sympathy for the French Revolution? If by clever explanations he can somehow be extricated from the charge of naked hypocrisy, does that show that his principles were so flexible and so subjective as to be readily adaptable to any situation? That all of his lofty talk about ethics was nothing but hot air, and totally useless as a guide to real life in times of crisis?

The extent to which the liberal churches contributed to the secularization of Germany (and of Europe and North America) by turning away from traditional, orthodox Christianity is little known by people who enjoy belittling Christianity – hence, a quote from Prof. Gene Veith might be appropriate. Speaking specifically of Germany, he says:

The attack on the Bible within Protestantism was the work of both textual scholars and theologians. By the 20th century, the higher criticism of the Old Testament, which undercut traditional ideas about the authorship and composition of the Bible, had already weakened the doctrine of biblical authority. By assuming that the biblical text and the events it describes are to be explained in naturalistic, scientific terms, historical-critical scholarship vitiated the Bible's status as supernatural revelation.[48]

Nineteenth-century church historian Philip Schaff wrote that Germany's renowned Tuebingen school of theology, a fountainhead of new ideas in Christianity, "proceeds from disbelief in the supernatural and miraculous as a philosophical impossibility, and tries to explain the gospel history and the apostolic history from purely natural causes like every other history."[49] To quote another source, "Because of the influence of modern philosophy and modern science, and particularly because of the philosophy of Immanuel Kant and his followers, modern Protestantism rejects traditional Protestantism."[50]

The problem of theological liberalism has greatly confused the question of what Christianity is – especially since secular historians who approach this subject (not to mention even less well-informed people) are all too often ignorant of the subject. It is incredible to them that a pastor, a bishop, a theologian, could speak of "God," "Christ," "faith," yet nevertheless be very far removed from the teachings of Christ and in fact introducing a new religion using familiar Christian vocabulary for different ends.

This new religion was based not on divine revelation but on human reason, and was nothing but humanistic philosophy using religious words and still trying to cling to some sort of groundless hope. In this new religious system, Christ was merely a great moral teacher with a "sublime" ethical system, nothing more. He did not die on the cross for the sins of the world, was not born of a virgin, and was not literally God in human form. The biblical Heaven and Hell and the Day of Judgment were dismissed as pre-scientific myths. If there was such a thing as heaven, surely all that was needed to get there was sincerity. Feeling, a vague sense of the infinite, was more important than doctrine, and "faith" was limited to what might seem plausible to an unbelieving world. The buildings, hymns, vestments and ceremonies remained, but much of the church was lifeless and dead.

More needs to be said about the philosophical underpinnings of a radically new approach to the interpretation of Scripture. It was assumed that the four gospels were not historically accurate, and of course not divinely inspired. The early Christians had preserved some of Christ's sayings and given their impressions and hopes concerning him, but the authentically historical Jesus was lost in the mists of antiquity. Higher truth was discovered by the exercise of human reason alone, especially human reason operating according to the highly creative speculations of Hegel and/or Kant. Later in the century Darwinism and other manifestations of scientism also had a great influence on the churches.[51]

For the new theologians, "The Hegelian method had proved itself to be the logic of reality."[52] Of David Friedrich Strauss, who thought that Christianity contained spiritual truths presented in the form of myths and legends, we read: "Hegel's philosophy had set him free, giving him a clear conception of the relationship of idea and reality, leading him to a higher plane of Christological speculation, and opening his eyes to the mystic interpretation of finitude and infinity, God and man"[53] (whatever that means). Strauss maintained that Jesus never rose from the dead at all, but nevertheless the myth of his resurrection carries a deep spiritual meaning that we can somehow derive benefit from. In a book written in 1872, *The Old Faith and the New*, Strauss asserted that Christianity was only a past cultural legacy, and that Germans today should place their faith in the laboratories, factories, and military power of the Reich.[54] What a stupid fool.

The "peculiar kind of rationalism inspired by Kant"[55] was also deeply influential. We cannot have direct experience of God or of the supernatural; supposedly miraculous events all had natural causes, and we can accept no miraculous event until those natural causes have been found; the Bible must be treated like any other ancient book; a real knowledge of the divine is forbidden to us. So Christoph Friedrich von Ammon reasoned "on the lines of Kant's *Kritik der reinen Vernunft.*" "As a disciple of Kant," Ammon also explained that there was no miracle of Jesus turning water into wine at Cana. The wine was a gift which Jesus had secretly brought, and the legend of the miracle was based on a misunderstanding.[56]

Brian Magee wrote of Kant that "he wrought more destruction against established religious ways of thinking than any other philosopher has ever done."[57] This seemingly extravagant statement is probably true, given Kant's deep influence on liberal Protestantism in Germany, which then spread to America and to England. That "the empirical world is all there is," while "spirit, God, magic, the occult" belong to a world off-limits to reason, and beyond what we can truly know – such beliefs of the so-called Enlightenment as exemplified by Kant's simple-minded trust in the power of his own intelligence did immense damage to the German churches. Not that we blame the churches' problems all on modern attempts at philosophy. The blame lies with people within the church who chose to accept such ideas, or at least passively tolerated those who did.

People with these clever new ideas stood in the pulpits and talked about "the Gospel" and "Christ" and "salvation." They spoke of "faith" and "the Word of God," celebrated Christmas and Easter, took communion, and sang hymns – but it was all emptiness. These deceptions – derived from unbelief, and finding expression in useless and worthless pseudo-religious philosophies – ate out the very heart of the church. Who is going to suffer martyrdom for a Christ we do not know much about, but who was not born of a virgin and did not rise from the dead? Who is going to suffer for a book of myths and legends? Our innate need for higher reality cannot be met by human philosophy using borrowed religious terminology to make itself seem spiritual.

The churches based on this were shallow and weak, and later events of German history revealed this weakness. These churches were also irrelevant. They had nothing to offer to lost and confused people seething with resentment, fear, hatred, pride, and revenge. Given that they had already abandoned the essentials of the faith, how could such church leaders withstand the pressures of the 20th century? Their hearts were in the world, they had been following the world for a long time, and there was no reason why they should not continue to follow it – especially when the forces of totalitarianism began to emerge.

The malleable, flexible and merely human God of liberal so-called Protestantism is easily accommodated to any and every worldly philosophy, as we can see not merely in Germany, but in America today. Schaff wrote that a leading liberal German "theologian" of the nineteenth century tried to explain the Gospel of John as the result not of eternal truth and divine revelation, but of a process of merely human literary evolution.[58] There is no need to be puzzled by the surrender of the German churches to Hitler. Their imposing edifices, their seminaries and church buildings were for the most part whitewashed tombs.

When Christ was on earth, his severest criticisms were directed not at thieves, drunkards, murderers, prostitutes, homosexuals or plain people living normally without God. They were directed at religious leaders that used a lot of religious language but placed a barrier between people and God. It was the theologians and the pastors and the bishops who taught the German people that wherever the answer to their problems might lie, it was not in the church. Who can derive any strength, comfort or meaning from the belief that Jesus did not rise from the dead at all, that the resurrection was just a story invented by the apostles because of their messianic hope?

The abject surrender of the "theologians" and the "scholars" to the forces of secularism had a serious impact on German culture. Near the end of the nineteenth century R. L. Dabney wrote, "While German scholarship has been busy with its labors, it has suffered almost a whole nation to lapse into a semi-heathenish condition."[59] The idea that Germany was a Christian country is a myth perpetrated by those who understand neither Christianity nor Germany. Many people in 19th-century Germany who called themselves "Catholics" or "Protestants" were referring to infant baptism, childhood education, and vague cultural associations – not to a real commitment to following Christ.

Historians who say that such and such a percentage of alleged Protestants voted for Hitler are not concerned with how many of those "Protestants" thought that the biblical miracles never occurred, that Darwin was right about the origins of life, and that Christ was a religious genius but a mere man nevertheless, a man who did not die for the sins of the world, and did not rise from the dead. Even a secular historian who discusses the German church only in passing wrote of German church membership in 1890 that "many who maintained their church membership did so from custom rather than from conviction," adding that such Christians were "apt to be susceptible . . . to the challenge of science and the tendency toward modernism that had resulted from textual criticism of the sacred writings." He adds that church membership "was decreasing year by year."[60]

This rejection of scripture led the "Christians" in Nazi Germany into two directions. Some tried to maintain their outward appearance of Christianity, even as they were careful never to cross any red lines and directly challenge the power or the doctrine of the state. Many of them even thought that the undeniable vitality of the Nazi movement would somehow redound to the benefit of Germany and the churches. They thought Hitler would bring about a national renewal from which all could gain. Needless to say, if they could have seen how things would end, they would have wanted nothing to do with Hitler.

Others whole-heartedly embraced Naziism and openly conformed their belief to the Nazi ideology. These were the so-called "Germanic

Christians" who declared (among other things) that God had created separate races, and that it was their Christian duty to follow Hitler and to keep the German race pure. Groups such as the Federation for a German Church, the Thuringian German Christians, and the German Christian Movement had been espousing Nazi-like ideas long before 1933. They eagerly turned to Hitler. Blaming the Jews for Germany's defeat in World War I; rejecting democracy and calling for a strong leader; seeking to remove Jewish influences from the Bible; rejecting the supposedly Jewish doctrine of original sin; redefining the cross as a symbol of struggle for National Socialism or human political sacrifice; stating that God had sent Hitler and that a new revelation was to be found in him – none of this has anything to do with any teachings of Christ. Nevertheless, some historians nowadays seem to enjoy linking the "Protestants" to Hitler. The "Protestants" voted for Hitler, Hitler did well in this "devoutly Protestant" area; even the pro-Nazi philosopher Heidegger – who did not believe in the Bible by the way – has been tied to his Protestant background.

This has contemporary relevance. It has been approximately ninety to one hundred years since destructive liberal theology gained control of the mainline denominations in America. This, along with other factors, has contributed greatly to our pronounced national decline – and many seminaries and churches are now in such a state that we can confidently predict there will be no resistance from them should the forces of evil manage to get control of the levers of power. Is the collapse of the churches before National Socialism any different from the beginning collapse of the churches before the forces of secularism today? Wouldn't Christians who effortlessly accommodate their faith to meet the demands of abortionists, radical feminists, and homosexual rights activists also have willingly embraced the equally false philosophies of Aryan supremacy and racial antisemitism? In denying Scripture, they open the door to any and every idea that might emerge out of the unbelieving world.

Thomas Oden's book *Requiem: A Lament in Three Movements* gives a striking picture of seminaries and church bureaucracies that have largely and even completely abandoned biblical Christianity and embraced the world. He speaks of "unprecedented mutations" in the church; of mockery of the Trinity and dismissal of the need for Christ's sacrificial death; of "overt advocacy of lesbianism as an acceptable and commended practice for Christian women"; of a communion service dedicated to the feminist goddess Sophia.[61] Does anyone imagine these people will stand for Christ in times of persecution? If we want to understand the strange silence of the German churches under Hitler we need only to look around us.

People who want to discuss these things should read more German history. Craig's history of modern Germany contains a brief yet insightful description of German Protestant theology towards the end of the nineteenth century. He writes that the leading theologians of Germany had yielded to the pressures of modernism, and "had long since abandoned the dogmatic rigour of an earlier age." Christianity was no longer considered to be divinely revealed, and scholarship that undermined the Bible led to "an incautious eagerness to adapt the beliefs of the Church to the latest fashions in scientific speculation."[62]

Protestantism in the end became "nothing but a bundle of ethical rules, inspired not by divine authority but by social utility."[63] And, if the main benefit of religion is not forgiveness of sin and eternal life but rather social utility, it is not hard to see what might happen when someone came along who promised to solve Germany's severe economic and political problems. It would naturally be the duty of religion to support him, for the good of the people. After all, if true religion is doing good, and tearing up the Versailles Treaty and restoring economic stability and national honor are good, there is no need for deeper reflection about vexing questions of right and wrong.

This is not to blame the collapse of the churches solely on theological modernism. Christians who are theoretically orthodox can also be part of the problem. There is after all such a thing as lifeless, spiritless, powerless orthodoxy. Much of today's theoretically orthodox evangelical and fundamentalist Christianity lacks power, commitment and authority. D. Martyn Lloyd-Jones wrote of this, saying, "Correct doctrine can leave the church dead; you can have dead orthodoxy, you can have a church that is perfectly orthodox but perfectly useless." Christ said, "Ye are the salt of the earth: but if the salt have lost his savour, wherewith shall it be salted? It is thenceforth good for nothing, but to be cast out, and to be trodden under foot of men" (Matthew 5:13). It must be said with sadness that there were churches in Nazi Germany, and there are churches in America today, that were and are good for nothing, that were and will be trodden under foot by men.

The Secular Origins of the Holocaust

[This article first appeared in the March/April 2012 (25.2) issue of *Touchstone: A Journal of Mere Christianity* (www.touchstonemag.com[1]). It was originally titled "From Modernity To Auschwitz: The Secular & Anti-Christian Origins of the Holocaust." It is used by agreement.]

In his lengthy book *The Holocaust in Historical Context*, Prof. Steven Katz of Boston University links biblical Christianity to the crimes of the Nazis. He recognizes the obvious fact that the Nazis weren't Christians, that they were in fact hostile to Christianity, but Katz still claims that centuries of Christian-inspired hatred of Jews, derived from the Bible, contributed indirectly but significantly to the murder of six million Jews. Christianity is thus blamed for creating a reservoir of hate that the non-Christian Hitler skillfully exploited.

Brought out by a major publisher (Oxford University Press) and praised by scholars from such top American universities as Yale and Cornell, Prof. Katz's book represents a common understanding of the relationship of Christianity to the Holocaust. To give one more example of many, Martin Gilbert's *The Holocaust: A History of the Jews of Europe During the Second World War*, begins with a reference to Martin Luther's anti-Semitism, as if that were the natural starting point for an understanding of these horrors. Other writers on the origins of the Holocaust have not been slow to link the crimes of the Nazis to earlier Medieval "Christian" anti-Semitism as well.

It does not take much time to demonstrate that the Bible does not teach hatred of Jews, or of anyone else. True, Paul spoke severely of the Jews in I Thessalonians, stating that "they please not God and are contrary to all men" – but in the same sentence he also condemns the Thessalonians ("for ye also have suffered like things of your own countrymen"). Jesus did call those who were plotting to kill him children of the devil (John 8:40, 44), but this is a general truth

---

applicable to any and all murderers. Pilate thought to acquit himself by washing his hands, but Scripture does not let him off so lightly, and involves Gentiles as well as Jews in the death of Christ (Acts 4:25-27).

"The Jews killed Christ – death to the Jews!" This is so far removed from all fundamental biblical teachings that we must reject any attempt to use such crimes to blacken the Gospel of Christ: and isn't this the underlying motive of many such accusations – hostility to the Christian message, and a desire to disparage it at every opportunity? Yet, there may be a deeper and a more subtle motive at work than simple bias against Christianity. Professor Zygmunt Bauman describes this motive in his thoughtful book *Modernity and the Holocaust*. It is a desire to avoid the fact that the Holocaust was a product of modernism – a troubling thought that calls into question the entire modernist project.

If we can blame the brutalities of Naziism to a significant extent on religion, then we do not have to confront Bauman's claim that "the Holocaust was a characteristically modern phenomenon that cannot be understood out of the context of cultural tendencies and technical achievements of modernity." Pointing at religion thus becomes (as he says) merely one way "to belittle, misjudge, or shrug off the significance of the Holocaust" – and the dream of modernity as progress guided by independent human reason remains untarnished.

If, however, we are not wedded (or chained?) to the modernist paradigm; if we do not feel obligated to defend our belief in the goodness of human nature; in the power of reason to order and improve society; and in the benefits of freedom from divine law; if we do not see Hitler's crimes as a religiously influenced deviation from an otherwise sound modern secular outlook – then we can consider the horrors of National Socialism in a different light.

A New Kind of Anti-Semitism

The 18th century saw the emergence of a powerful intellectual movement that denied the need for divine revelation, and boasted of the power of human reason unaided to create a better world. Optimistically named "the Enlightenment," this movement originated primarily in France, but was eagerly received in Germany as well. It was this "Enlightenment" that introduced a new and different way of looking at the Jews – one based on human reason, and integral to German anti-Semitism in the following generations.

The secular thinkers of the German "Enlightenment" (*Aufklaerung*), of whom we may take Immanuel Kant as a prime example, were not concerned about God's wrath on the Jews for their rejection of Christ. Such a concept of God was alien to them. Their concerns were very different, and their increasingly strident objections to Jews were different. To begin with, it was the concept of Judaism itself, as secular thinkers found it in Torah, that offended them. A God of one nation only, who imposed all sorts of stifling rules and regulations, who rewarded obedience with material blessings, and visited severe punishments for various sins, was anathema to those who, like Kant, felt that human civilization had outgrown the need for such divine tutelage. Moreover, verses such as Genesis 28:20-21 were used to show that the main concern of the Jews was selfish advantage and material benefit, not a disinterested love of truth for its own sake.

Related to the charge of selfishness and materialism was Kant's accusation that the Jews had no real emphasis on the afterlife. Missing clear references in the Jewish scriptures to an afterlife (such as Isaiah 51:6 or Daniel 12:2-3, to name only two), Kant accused the Jews of being concerned with this life only. As he wrote in *Religion within the Limits of Reason Alone*, "... since no religion can be conceived of which involves no belief in a future life, Judaism, which, when taken in its purity is seen to lack this belief, is not a religious faith at all." Thus, when Hitler wrote in *Mein Kampf* ". . . he [the Jew] lacks idealism in any form, and hence belief in a hereafter is absolutely foreign to him," he was not expressing ideas derived from the older religious anti-Semitism, but from a newer tradition (by Hitler's time such arguments were widely diffused throughout the culture).

Thirdly, the obstinacy with which the Jews clung to their outmoded beliefs in defiance of Western civilization's obvious progress was taken by Kant as evidence that the Jews were an inferior people, isolated from essential aspects of the human experience, and even from basic human feeling. Jewish participants in the "Enlightenment" such as Moses Mendelssohn, who might have been embraced by Kant, were later accused by more extreme anti-Semites of merely copying, or feeding parasitically off of, the superior Western civilization to which the oriental Jews would forever be outsiders.

Kant's contribution here is too little appreciated. This dominant figure of secular and enlightened German culture was deeply hostile to Jews, and his influence during the following century was great. As Paul Lawrence Rose wrote in *Wagner: Race and Revolution,* "Kant's basic ideas were elaborated into a historical and philosophical critique of Judaism that until very recently commanded virtually unquestioning support in German culture."

Kant was not a racial anti-Semite – that twist would emerge later in the 19th century – and no doubt he would have vehemently repudiated later excesses: but Prof. Michael Mack's book *German Idealism and the Jew: The Inner Anti-Semitism of Philosophy and German Jewish Responses* demonstrates Kant's contribution to a new way of thinking about Jews. This rational, philosophical anti-Semitism was to be carried on, amplified, and intensified by such later thinkers as Fichte, Schopenhauer, Wagner, and H. S. Chamberlain (the last two of these have been consistently linked to Hitler).

Kant's ethics are also relevant to this topic. His famous Categorical Imperative, which sought a rational rather than a divine basis for ethics, could readily be adopted to meet the demands of anyone in any situation. Thus, it could be reasoned: "Jews are a menace to humanity. If everyone did as I did and killed Jews, society would benefit. Therefore, killing Jews is ethical." This sort of thinking was not Kant's intention, but once the barriers of divine law and judgment are removed, anything is possible. In the words of Christian apologist John Montgomery, "Kant separated ethics from theology, morals from God: this he believed to be one of his greatest contributions; in fact, it was one of his greatest mistakes" (*Tractatus Logico-Theologicus*).

Parenthetically, Kant was also a racist, and openly declared that "Humanity is at its greatest perfection in the race of the whites" (*Physical Geography*). He first strongly condemned war, but then qualified his condemnation by stating that, at our present level of development, war was a necessary agent of progress, and had certain cultural benefits (a vital element of later German militarism). This was in *An Answer to the Question: "What is Enlightenment?"* – a book which also disparaged English democracy as a fraud and extolled the greater freedom enjoyed by Germans under the authoritarian Prussian kings. This concept of finding real freedom by obeying the leader readily lent itself to harmful extremes.

Kant dismissed traditional religious faith as "laziness and cowardice" and called on people to have the courage to walk by reason alone. But, there were disturbing aspects to Kant's peculiar brand of "rationality" – aspects that were to be added to and developed in ways he himself could not have imagined.

Hostility to Jewish-inspired Christianity

Kant was outwardly respectful of Christianity, even as he denied its central teachings, but German thinkers were to become increasingly hostile to Christianity's un-Germanic and unenlightened values as the century progressed. Arthur Schopenhauer, for example, writing mostly in the first half of the 19th century, condemned belief in divine revelation as childish (*Religion: A Dialogue*). He also objected to Christianity's Jewish influence on Europe.

Schopenhauer wrote in *The World as Will and Idea* that "... it is to be regarded generally as a great misfortune that the people whose culture was to be the basis for our own were not the Indians or the Greeks, but these very Jews." In his view, the arbitrary separation of mankind from the animal world by the myth of a divine creation was especially harmful. "Christianity contains, in fact, a great and essential imperfection in limiting its precepts to man, and in refusing rights to the animal world . . . Such are the effects of the first chapter of Genesis, and, in fact, of the whole Jewish conception of nature" (*Religion: A Dialogue*).

Raising Kant's objection that the Jews were materialists incapable of any spiritual life, Schopenhauer also claimed that the Jews had corrupted sound Christian teachings that had first originated in India. Moreover, he described the Jews as "a sneaking dirty race afflicted with filthy diseases," and saw them as an obstacle to Germany's moral and cultural development. He thought that Judaism should be eliminated, but this was to be accomplished by assimilation – so he advocated granting civil rights to the Jews, thinking their merging with society would lead over time to their disappearance.

That Christianity was both Jewish in origin and character, and also incompatible with the supposedly stronger and healthier values of pre-Christian German paganism, became an increasingly common theme. Paul Lagarde, an influential leader of the imperialistic and militaristic Folkish movement in pre-WWI Germany, sought to purify an originally Indian "Aryan Christianity" of its later Jewish accretions, and saw traditional Christianity (along with pacifism, democracy, and liberalism) as corrupting the purity of the German soul. Lagarde saw Jewish / Christian influence as totally incompatible with Germany's spiritual mission to lead the way in the upward progress of mankind, and called for the Jews to be exterminated.

Julius Langbehn, a best-selling author and also a leader in the Folkish movement, saw the Jews in the same way. He equated them with disease, and advocated that they be exterminated – and these views were not mere eccentricities, but became increasingly popular in certain segments of the German intelligentsia. Historian George Mosse, quoting Fritz Stern, writes, ". . . a thousand teachers in republican Germany who in their youth had worshipped Lagarde or Langbehn were just as important in the triumph of National Socialism as all the putative millions of marks that Hitler collected from the German tycoons" (*The Crisis of German Ideology: Intellectual Origins of the Third Reich*).

The most extreme statement of this hostility to Jewish Christianity can be found in Nietzsche's book *The Antichrist.* There we read, after a long and bitter blast against the falsehood, dishonesty, cowardice, and corruption of Christianity, that it is essentially a Jewish religion. "… the Christian church, put beside the 'people of God,' shows a complete lack of any claim to originality" (section 24); ". . . the small insurrectionary movement which took the name of Jesus of Nazareth is simply the Jewish instinct redivivus. . . " (27); ". . . in primitive Christianity one finds only concepts of a Judaeo-Semitic character" (32); "One would as little choose 'early Christians' for companions as Polish Jews … Neither has a pleasant smell" (46). He dismissed Christians as "little super-Jews, ripe for some sort of madhouse" (44) and added "The Christian is simply a Jew of the 'reformed' confession" (44).

Nietzsche went on to claim that Christianity was a Jewish plot, cooked up by the rabbi Paul as a means of undermining the Roman empire and enslaving stronger and morally superior people with groundless fears of sin, conscience, the day of judgment, God, and other such Jewish tricks. These ideas are found in sections 22, 24, and 43, to name only three of many places where these themes are harped on at length. "To the sort of men who reach out for power under Judaism and Christianity – that is to say, to the priestly class –

decadence is no more than a means to an end. Men of this sort have a vital interest in making mankind sick" (24). In this passage Nietzsche calls the Jews master manipulators of decadence. "Precisely for this reason the Jews are the most *fateful* people in the history of the world: their influence has so falsified the reasoning of mankind . . ." (24)

It is significant that while Nietzsche and Hitler were obviously different in many ways, their views of Christianity were identical. In his *Table Talk*, accepted as genuine by historians, Hitler referred to Christianity as a Jewish invention, a rebellion of the weak against the strong that led to the collapse of the Roman Empire, invented by the apostle Paul (who falsified Christ's teachings). Like Nietzsche, Hitler saw Christianity as against natural law, a force for social disintegration, a religion of failures and losers, contrary to science, a device for priests to hold power over people (for the sake of brevity quotes from Nietzsche on these and yet other points were omitted).

Robert Wistrich's comments in *Hitler and the Holocaust: How and Why the Holocaust Happened* are insightful here. He writes that Hitler blamed the Jews for unhealthy and unnatural Judaeo-Christian ethics, and saw them as the prime source of "contemporary teachings of pacifism, equality before God and the law, human brotherhood and compassion for the weak, which Naziism had to uproot." Unfortunately, too few people realize that hostility to Christianity was a key element in the concept of Jews as destroyers of culture and deadly enemies of the German people.

Contempt for Human Life

With the loss of the biblical teaching of the immortal human soul created by God, devaluation of human life is inevitable and inescapable. This trend was already evident in German philosophy in the first half of the 19th century and found clear expression in the philosophy of Hegel (though Fichte, Schopenhauer, and others could also be mentioned in this context).

The introduction of Darwin's theories greatly accelerated an already existing trend (Schopenhauer asserted in *The Horrors and Absurdities of Religion* that "Man is at bottom a dreadful wild animal . . . man is a beast of prey") – but Darwinism gave scientific approval to the belief that the individual was insignificant, a mere speck in a vast and remorseless progression in which only the survival and advancement of the species mattered.

Many German thinkers went far beyond the mere acceptance of Darwinism as an explanation for life as we know it, and used the revolutionary new theory as a basis for ethical and philosophical speculation as well. The clearest single example of this trend (though many others could be named) is the German biologist Ernst Haeckel. A tireless propagandist for Darwinism, he ridiculed Christianity as outmoded superstition, and presented scientific rationalism as the only sure path to truth.

Attempting to follow the logical implications of Darwinism for human ethics led Haeckel into deep and troubled waters. For one thing, he concluded that "the struggle for life" was the iron law of existence (this in his best-selling book *The Riddle of the Universe*). This struggle was morally blind, indifferent, and knew only survival or extinction. By a swift sleight of hand Haeckel elevated this struggle from the level of biological species to that of nations and races. Thus, if a stronger country seized territory from a weaker one, or a stronger race replaced a weaker one, or even exterminated it, this was nothing but survival of the fittest, evolution being worked out in our own day and time.

This fit naturally with the concept of racial purity. As the French thinker Arthur de Gobineau argued in his book *Essay on the Inequality of Human Races* (1853-55), racially pure races rose and dominated. When infected with impurity of blood, dominant races sickened and declined. Gobineau's book had a significant influence in Germany (he identified the Aryans as the most advanced and superior race), and the purity of German blood became a matter of national survival (a theme elaborated on by numbers of German thinkers).

The individual personality was lost in great evolutionary schemes stretching out over eons, and Haeckel claimed that the human "soul" disappeared at death, being merely an aspect of physical existence. Free will was also denied, there was only natural law to which humans were bound just as much as the animals (humans were animals). Christian ethics were dismissed as based on unscientific mythology, and if animals or people starved or perished miserably this was merely the natural state of affairs, a necessary aspect of the evolutionary process. To resist this was contrary to nature: as Nietzsche said in the *Antichrist*, "Pity thwarts the whole law of evolution, which is the law of natural selection" (7).

Individual human life was of little or no value. As Haeckel wrote in his *Riddle of the Universe*, human nature "has no more value for the universe at large than the ant, the fly of a summer's day, the microscopic infusorium, or the smallest bacillus." Not surprisingly, Haeckel was an early advocate of euthanasia, and felt that useless burdens on society such as defective infants, the insane, or the incurably ill should be killed. Surprisingly, Haeckel endorsed the Golden Rule, though he derived its validity not from God, but from evolution, which mandated social cooperation for survival of the group. The rule of love and kindness did not apply to enemies outside the group, however, nor did it apply to those within the group who were useless or defective.

Haeckel had a strong sense of hierarchy, and while human life as a whole was worth little, some people were higher on the evolutionary scale and so worth more than others. At the top were the white Europeans, especially the Germanic peoples. European colonialism was thoroughly justified – the stronger and more advanced ruled by the right of evolutionary law – and the lives of primitive and backward

Asian and African peoples were worth less than the lives of Europeans. This provided a scientific justification for militarism and imperialism, and Haeckel was not slow to make the connection. He felt that a German victory in World War I with substantial territorial acquisitions was the solution to Germany's shortage of "living space," and his exhortations to German soldiers to fight and die bravely for the Fatherland provide an interesting example of secular Darwinist militarism. This combined with political authoritarianism (nature shows us the rule of the strongest and the best, not parliamentary squabbling) to make Haeckel an example of how ideas that seem obviously wrong to us were respectable and widespread fifty years and more before Hitler came to power.

Haeckel's ideas have been presented briefly here, and much more could have been said. Prof. Richard Weikart's book *From Darwin to Hitler: Evolutionary Ethics, Eugenics, and Racism in Germany* describes in detail the impact of Darwin-based philosophizing on the German intelligentsia, and shows how widespread such ideas were. *The Scientific Origins of National Socialism* by Prof. Daniel Gasman focuses specifically on Haeckel. In spite of their different approaches and emphases, both authors make the point that some of Hitler's ideas sound as if they had been taken verbatim from Haeckel.

The False God of Nationalism

The reliance on human wisdom alone did not only lead to new approaches to "the Jew" and to ethics – it also led, in the German context, to a new concept of the nation. Where do we derive our sense of belonging, of significance, of eternity, if not from Christianity? Johann Gottlieb Fichte found it in the nation.

It was perhaps inevitable that with the loss of God, the nation should come to be seen as a substitute. Large enough and important enough to appeal to our need for a higher cause, yet real enough to be grasped by the natural mind, the welfare and advancement of the nation was seen more and more as the highest aim and ideal. Fichte is a striking example of this.

In his *Addresses to the German Nation*, Fichte (writing in the Napoleonic era) saw the nation as "the manifestation of divinity." The development of the national character was "the highest law in the spiritual world," "the rule of law and divine order." The vague "Absolute" or higher spiritual force of German idealist philosophy worked through national groups to achieve the advancement of mankind – and the purest race, the one most in harmony with that higher reality, was the German race.

Destined to lead mankind on its ascent to moral perfection, it was the German People, the *Volk*, that provided individual Germans with hope, meaning, purpose, and even eternal life. The individual dies, but the Fatherland lives. We need a sense of permanence, and "this permanence is promised to the individual by the continuous and independent existence of his nation" (*Addresses*). Hitler also said "What is life? Life is the Nation. The individual must die anyway. Beyond the life of the individual is the Nation." This way of thinking did not come from the

Christian heritage – and some of Fichte's writings survive from Hitler's personal library, heavily lined in places by his distinctive markings.

Fichte believed that the Germanic peoples of Europe should be united, that arbitrary boundaries dividing the German People should be removed. Hitler's goal of bringing all Germans "home to the Reich" was not a personal eccentricity but a common theme of 19th-century German nationalists. Fichte also felt that the Volk should be purified of unhealthy alien influences. Germany needed to preserve its unique virtues unmixed so it could continue its mission of "pointing the way to the regeneration of the human race." This desire for cultural and ethnic purity included a deep hatred of Jews as aliens corrupting and contaminating The People from within (unlike the French, who contaminated it from without). This concept of cultural pollution was later combined with the concept of racial pollution.

Fichte's *Contribution to the Correct Understanding of the French Revolution* (1793) is outspoken in its hostility to Jews – and his reasoning was not primarily that of traditional religious anti-Semitism. Greed, selfishness, materialism, alienation from the lofty spirit of the German People, hostility to the noble and pure German character – these were some Kantian themes with the addition of a nationalistic virulence unknown to the more genuinely cosmopolitan Kant.

It was in reference to such ideas that the 19th-century Jewish poet Heinrich Heine uttered his oft-quoted prophecy about the collapse of Christianity before a revived paganism, the "brutal Germanic lust for battle" that Christianity had only tamed but not eliminated. When Heine spoke of a revived Thor smashing the Gothic cathedrals with his giant hammer, he was referring specifically to the repudiation of traditional values he saw in "Kantian criticism, Fichtean transcendental idealism, and even *Naturphilosophie*" (which stressed union with fundamental powers of Nature rather than submission to divine law). Heine's work *On the History of Religion and Philosophy in Germany* shows a much profounder insight into the origins of National Socialism than do most writers who have the advantage of hindsight.

The wider abandonment of traditional Christianity as the 19th century progressed left a spiritual void, a deepening moral and cultural vacuum. Nationalism began to increasingly emerge in Germany as a substitute – and from exaltation of the nation, it is a short and simple step to exaltation of the leader of the nation in a manner totally inconceivable in a Christian context.

The Failure of Human Reason

Racism, militarism, imperialism, euthanasia, political authoritarianism, and new themes of anti-Semitism – such were the fruits of men who rejected the bible and relied solely on their own intelligence. All of this being so, we can only speculate about the motives of historian Richard Evans, when in his book *The Coming of the Third Reich* he tries to link the Nazi policy of euthanasia to "Protestant charities" whose "doctrines of predestination and original sin" led them to embrace Nazi practices including forced sterilization – as if euthanasia or any other such modern innovations had ever been practiced or even heard of in Calvin's Geneva or Knox's Scotland.

People as essentially animals locked in a pitiless and amoral struggle; traditional ethics derived from Christianity dismissed as useless fictions; loss of individual identity leading to membership in the national group as the source of identity and self worth; looking on sick and dying masses of people as a natural and healthy means of weeding out the unfit; Aryan supremacy; belief in a scientifically and rationally ordered community; Jews as a threat to a mythical racial purity, plotting to control the world – these and other modern secular ideas combined with various historical and social factors to make the Holocaust not inevitable, but possible.

These ideas did not emerge out of Christianity. They emerged out of the rejection of Christianity, and flourished in the intellectual and spiritual void created by modernism – and why shouldn't we use the hair and skin of dead people, if they are nothing but animals? Why not leave the sick, the weak, the inferior to perish miserably if that's just the way things are?

Much more could have been said about other German thinkers, especially Richard Wagner and H.S. Chamberlain, whose views were in many ways close to or even identical to Hitler's. More could have been said about such aspects as the masterful use of modern bureaucracy and technology to rationally and logically achieve detestable ends – but those ends were conceived in the realms of thought, thought based on the wisdom of the world, and the repudiation of the Christian religion. As Christ said, "If the light that is in thee be darkness, how great is that darkness?"

Nietzsche's Philosemitic Anti-Judaism

[This article first appeared in the May/June 2018 (31.3) issue of *Touchstone: A Journal of Mere Christianity* (www.touchstonemag.com[1]), originally titled "The Great Jewish Plot: The Riddle of Nietzsche's Philosemitic Anti-Judaism." It is used by agreement.]

Friedrich Nietzsche's overt hostility toward and contempt for Christianity were unusual in his day, but in the following century they have become more common. Nowadays Nietzsche has become something of a cultural icon, and his beliefs that Christianity is not merely false, but unnatural, harmful, and hostile to life are becoming more normative than many Christians realize.

The reasons for Nietzsche's hatred of Christianity – and "hatred" is not too strong a word here – are not always fully grasped. Far from being the result of a dispassionate and reasoned consideration of facts and evidence, Nietzsche's approach to the Christian religion was influenced not only by various personal issues that may never be fully explained, but also by a deep hostility toward Jews and toward Judaism.

Many people agree with Nietzsche that there is no God, and that supposedly divine rules are merely human inventions, leaving us free to follow our own inclinations to the furthest limit, without let or restraint. Such ideas are sweet music to the ears of those who desire only personal freedom without regard for future consequences – but some who agree with Nietzsche's anti-religious conclusions would not share the unusual thought processes by which he reached those conclusions. In particular, his conviction that Christianity was merely a Jewish trick, invented to enslave stronger peoples with a false slave morality, would be difficult for even the most articulate atheist to cogently defend today.

Apart from the larger question of a noted and highly influential contemporary thinker's attitude toward Christianity, there is the secondary issue of Nietzsche's still debated role in the emergence of National Socialist ideology. Nietzsche's strong condemnations of antisemitism, as well as his favorable comments about individual Jews and even about the Old Testament, have been widely effective in distancing Nietzsche from the horrors of later German history. If Nietzsche condemned democracy and called for the rule of an elite few; if he endorsed slavery and glorified war and violence; if he provided many quotes which, taken at face value, did seem to mesh perfectly with Nazi ideology – still, his positive comments about Jews and his negative comments about antisemites make it much more difficult to link him to the Nazi ideologues who quoted him so freely.

It is too little realized that comments of Nietzsche's which appear to distance him from modern antisemitism are not always what they seem. Nietzsche's meanings are not always obvious, to be picked up easily just off the surface, and that is the case here. If occasional seemingly favorable comments about Jews can in fact be reconciled with more consistently negative ones, it might help towards a re-evaluation of Nietzsche's place in modern secular antisemitism.

Take, for example, Nietzsche's praise of the Jewish Scriptures. In *The Genealogy of Morals*, Nietzsche asserts his distaste for the New Testament, and goes on to say "all honour to the Old Testament. I find therein great men, an heroic landscape . . . further still, I find a people" (BGE III, 22).[64] Certainly a conventional antisemite would never have praised Judaism in this way – but then, Nietzsche was never conventional, and it is a common mistake to read him too superficially.

To begin with, Nietzsche was after all an atheist, and the idea of a God laying down laws and rules with punishments for disobedience and rewards for obedience was anathema to him. Moreover, in *The Antichrist* Nietzsche explicitly denounced the Old Testament, saying "The concept of God falsified; the concept of morality falsified: but the

Jewish priesthood did not stop at this . . . These priests accomplished that miracle of falsification, of which the greater part of the Bible is the document" (AC 26)[65].

To understand how Nietzsche could praise a (to him) fundamentally false book that contradicted his most basic tenets, we need only to look back to Ludwig Feuerbach. This early atheist asserted that conventionally religious concepts of God were merely projections of human consciousness; that religion was false, yet still significant as a profound human expression of aspirations toward justice and meaning in life. In the same way, Nietzsche could dismiss the Old Testament as false in "the greater part," yet still see the remainder, with its conquests, wars, and "the mighty and thoroughly free-born figures of the history of Israel" (AC 26) as the expression of a healthy consciousness.

"Originally, and above all in the period of the kings, even Israel's attitude to all things was the *right one* – that is to say, the natural one. Its Jehovah was the expression of its consciousness of power, of its joy over itself, of its hope for itself" (AC 25). This is contrasted in the same section however with the later transformation (which he elaborates on) from an originally healthy Jewish concept of God allowing for power, conquest and victory, to one cunningly devised by priests for their own advantage. This new concept of God imposed "a so-called moral order of the universe," including guilt, obedience, punishments and rewards – all of which Nietzsche blasted with great hostility. So, Nietzsche's praise of the Old Testament is merely praise for that part of it which, though untrue, allows for "healthy" manifestations of the will-to-power, while "the greater part" of it is condemned as a harmful fabrication which Nietzsche later blames directly for the emergence of Christianity.

Other comments of Nietzsche's about the Jews also do not hold up under careful analysis. For example, in *Beyond Good and Evil,* Nietzsche states that "The Jews, however, are beyond all doubt the strongest, toughest and purest race at present living in Europe; they know how to prevail even under the worst conditions" (BGE VIII, 251)[66]. This may seem like very high praise, except Hitler also wrote of the remarkable endurance and racial toughness of the Jews in *Mein Kampf* (volume I, chapter 11, "Nation and Race"): "In hardly any people in the world is the instinct of self-preservation developed more strongly than in the so-called 'chosen.' Of this, the mere fact of the survival of this race may be considered the best proof... What people, finally, has gone through greater upheavals than this one – and nevertheless emerged from the mightiest catastrophes of mankind unchanged? What an infinitely tough will to live and preserve the species speaks from these facts!"[67] This interest in the strange survival of the Jewish people was not just a mania of Hitler's, but was a common theme among secular antisemites who did not accept a personal God's will and purpose in human affairs.

It is interesting that the above quote from *Beyond Good and Evil* shows Nietzsche's recognition of the importance of racial purity. He did not elevate race to a central position in his thought, but he did have an interest in it, and mentioned racial matters a number of times in his works. In *The Genealogy of Morals* alone we find references to "the stronger races" (II, 13); "a means to the purification of the race" (II, 13); the harmful effects of race-mixing ("the result of the crossing of too heterogeneous races", III, 17); "race decay" and "degeneration" (II, 19); the triumph of Judaism possibly due to blood poisoning (I, 9); and the "fundamental instinct of a higher dominant race" (I, 2). More references could have been given.

Another favorable comment Nietzsche made about the Jews needs to be carefully examined. He wrote the following in *Beyond Good and Evil* (VIII, 251): "That the Jews *could*, if they wanted – or if they were compelled, as the anti-Semites seem to want – even now predominate, indeed quite literally rule over Europe, is certain; that they are *not* planning and working towards that is equally certain."

Claiming that the Jews could rule Europe if they chose to do so shows that Nietzsche saw "the Jews" as a vague and mysterious entity of hidden and secret powers. This has ominous implications that we can easily see in retrospect – and does anyone today want to maintain that nineteenth-century Jewish scholars, merchants, rabbis, and common people had the power to rule Europe? If they had really been so powerful, surely they could have prevented a pogrom or two, or at least won a first acquittal for Alfred Dreyfus. Nietzsche here inhabits a twilight world of serious misconceptions. Such misconceptions are not merely nonsensical – they are also dangerous.

This quote illustrates that Nietzsche had a very peculiar way of looking at the Jews – and for someone who changed his mind about Richard Wagner completely and went from high praise for the man to bitter reviling, it is a small step from "are not planning and working" to "are planning and working." That Nietzsche was headed in this direction just before his collapse into complete insanity is evident from a comment he made in *The Antichrist*, where he says of the Jews that "with a *non plus ultra* of histrionic genius, they have known how to set themselves at the head of all decadent movements (St Paul and Christianity for instance)" (AC 24). It is not that the Jews are decadent themselves, but rather that they use decadence for their own ends. Motivated by resentment against "life, prosperity, power, beauty, and self-affirmation" they have "a vital interest in making men sick" (AC 24). Thus, in Nietzsche's view, "all decadent movements" are the result of Jewish machinations.

For one more example of a seemingly positive quote about Jews, we note in *Beyond Good and Evil* that Jews – who have "the genius of money and patience" – could be bred with Germans, who have "the hereditary art of commanding and obeying." This was part of Nietzsche's plan for "the breeding of a new ruling caste for Europe" (BGE VIII, 251). Apart from the profoundly undemocratic as well as the imaginary nature of this speculation, we note that the Jews are considered from a peculiar perspective that denies them individuality and humanity.

Nietzsche could accept and even praise individual Jews such as Heine, Spinoza, or others who had somehow emancipated themselves from false concepts of God and morality – but for the Jewish people as a whole, and for their influence through Christianity on the development of Western culture, Nietzsche had a distorted and malevolent hatred. Perhaps the simplest way to bring this into focus is to point out that Nietzsche blamed the collapse of the Roman Empire, the Protestant Reformation, and the French Revolution on Jewish influence.

Concerning the Roman Empire, we read in *The Genealogy of Morals* that the noble, superior, aristocratic and healthy values of rapaciously imperialistic and warlike Rome were undermined by "the Jew," whom Nietzsche saw as "the incarnation of the unnatural . . . in Rome the Jew was held to be *convicted of hatred* of the whole human race; and rightly so" (GM I, 16). After rhapsodizing on the glories of Rome ("every relic of them, every inscription enraptures"), Nietzsche goes on to ask "Which of them has been provisionally victorious, Rome or Judaea? But there is not a shadow of doubt . . . not only in Rome, but almost over half the world, everywhere man has been tamed or is about to be tamed" people bow down "to *three Jews*, as we know, and *one Jewess* (to Jesus of Nazareth, to Peter the fisher, to Paul the tentmaker, and to the mother of the aforesaid Jesus, named Mary . . . Rome is undoubtedly defeated" (GM I, 16) [italics Nietzsche's].

At this point it is necessary to explain that Nietzsche considered Christianity to be synonymous with Judaism. This is manifest in some quotes from *The Antichrist*: "the Christian church, put beside the 'people of God,' shows a complete lack of any claim to originality" (AC 24); "the small insurrectionary movement christened with the name of Jesus of Nazareth is simply the Jewish instinct *over again*" (AC 27); "early Christianity deals only in Judaeo-Semitic conceptions"

(AC 32); "We should feel just as little inclined to hobnob with 'the first Christians' as with Polish Jews: not that we need explain our objections . . . They simply smell bad. – In vain have I sought for a single sympathetic feature in the New Testament" (AC 46) [ellipsis in the original].

Thus, when Nietzsche says "Christianity was the vampire of the *imperium Romanum*, - in a night it shattered the stupendous achievement of the Romans"; when in this context he describes Christians as acting "disintegratingly, poisonously and witheringly, like *blood-suckers*" (AC 58); in all of these and many other hate-filled comments, he is talking about Jews. Here we have the clearest possible description of Jews as bloodsuckers and vampires, using Christianity as a weapon to undermine what is truly good and noble, motivated by hatred and the desire for revenge. "Paul, with the logician's cynicism of a rabbi . . . St Paul, the Chandala hatred against Rome, against 'the world,' the Jew, the eternal Jew *par excellence*, become flesh and genius" (AC 44, 58) – this was the reason for the fall of marvelous and wonderful Rome.

In the same passage of *Genealogy of Morals* where Nietzsche gives his theories about the fall of Rome, he asserts that the Protestant Reformation was also a "movement of revenge" in which "Judaea triumphed again" (GM 1, 16). To Nietzsche, the reassertion of Jewish-Christian biblical values over the splendor of the Renaissance (see also AC 61) was merely the revolt of vulgar and low people against their aristocratic betters, inspired by Jewish values of democracy and equality that were hostile to unrestrained assertions of power by a social elite.

Still in the same section of *The Genealogy of Morals*, we read that the French Revolution was the result of the insidious and corrupting influence of the Jews. "Judaea proved yet once more victorious over the classical ideal of the French Revolution." The destruction of "the last political aristocracy that existed in Europe, that of the *French* seventeenth and eighteenth centuries, broke into pieces under the instincts of a resentful populace." Nietzsche's ideal of "the aristocratic, the powerful, the high-stationed, the high-minded" (GM I, 2) succumbed to "the will to lowliness, abasement, and equalization" (GM I, 16) of which the Jews were the most clever manipulators.

Few historians today would see the pampered and luxurious French nobility as representative of any sort of "classical ideal," and few would accept that the hidden hand of the Jew lay behind such widely disparate historical and social movements as the fall of the Roman Empire, the Reformation, and the French Revolution - but Nietzsche has never been renowned for his knowledge of European history. What is significant is the view of the Jews as the underlying source of Europe's spiritual and moral decline from the heights of a morally unfettered paganism. This outlook was by no means unique to Nietzsche.

If we understand that Jewish influence was synonymous with Christian influence, and that "Christian influence" meant not literal adherence to the teachings of Jesus, but rather the generally bourgeois European culture that had evolved out of a strongly Christian background, ideas of Europe having succumbed to Jewish influence seem less peculiar. What might otherwise seem like the ravings of lunatics in padded cells actually turns out to have a certain weird kind of logic. We can understand how it was possible to blame the Jews for both communism and capitalism, for atheism and Christianity, for the Reformation and the French Revolution, degenerate modern art, democracy, rootless cosmopolitanism, pacifism, and failure to sufficiently appreciate Wagner's operas.

But how can this deeply negative emphasis be reconciled with unequivocal condemnations of antisemitism? Nietzsche's condemnations are not as comprehensive or as unqualified as they are commonly thought to be. Here, as is so often the case with Nietzsche, a simple explanation is inadequate. He was condemning antisemites because they had a superficial understanding that did not get to the root of the problem.

Conventional religious antisemitism was of no use to Nietzsche. He did not see the Jews as under divine judgment for having crucified the Son of God. Jesus was to him only a man with highly dubious values. Nietzsche's sympathies were with Pontius Pilate, as he explained in *The Antichrist*: "Do I require to add that in the whole of the New Testament only *one* figure appears which we cannot help respecting? Pilate, the Roman Governor . . . One Jew more or less – what did it matter?" (AC 46).

This applies not merely to religious antisemites, but to philosophical and seemingly secular antisemites as well. Nietzsche saw German philosophy as also having been infected by Jewish Christianity, because of its emphasis on higher and unseen spiritual dimensions to reality. As he wrote in *The Antichrist*: ". . . philosophy is ruined by the blood of theologians. The Protestant minister is the grandfather of German philosophy . . . to understand what German philosophy really is at bottom, *i.e.*: - theology *in disguise* . . . Kant's success is merely a theologian's success" (AC 10).

Kant, Hegel, Fichte and many others did not accept the literal truth of the Bible in any sense, yet in their assertion (as Nietzsche saw it) of a higher reality of spirit, and conventional ideas of the reality of truth and virtue, they were in Nietzsche's view still contaminated with Judaism. As Nietzsche so succinctly put it: "It is necessary to state whom we regard as our antithesis: - the theologians, and all those who have the blood of the theologians in their veins – the whole of our philosophy" (AC 8, 10).

This makes it possible to understand Nietzsche's attacks on antisemites in a different way. While professing to oppose Judaism, they were still under its influence. That people should claim to be against the Jews while they themselves were enthralled by Jewish-Christian values, or to what Nietzsche thought were

Jewish-Christian values, was to Nietzsche simply ridiculous, and excited his deepest anger. For example, Nietzsche's contemptuous but brief dismissal of Wagner's antisemitism in *Nietzsche Contra Wagner* was made only in passing. The bulk of his argument consists of long denunciations of Wagner for having expressed what Nietzsche took to be Christian values in his opera *Parsifal*. That Wagner should purport to be an antisemite while at the same time advocating what Nietzsche thought to be a form of Jewish Christianity was unendurable to Nietzsche. It was Wagner's supposed "collapse before the cross" that provoked an ailing and troubled Nietzsche's fury.

Nietzsche's conflation of religion with philosophy, of Christian and secular philosophical antisemitisms, can be seen in *The Genealogy of Morals*, where Nietzsche says: "I like not, again, these newest speculators in idealism, the Anti-Semites, who nowadays roll their eyes in the patent Christian-Aryan-man-of-honour fashion" (GM III, 26). Antisemites who purported to uphold the values of Christianity, or of idealistic values derived from the belief in a higher spiritual reality, even a non-Christian one, were to Nietzsche at best useless, at worst contemptible and ridiculous. That they should pride themselves on their Aryan and Germanic heritage while adulterating it with Jewish values of morality, duty, and the higher "truths" of idealistic philosophy, while failing to return to the healthy and warlike virtues of "the dominant blondes, the Aryan conquering race" (GM I, 5) – this aroused that anger in Nietzsche that was never far beneath the surface.

This adds a significant new strain to European anti-Judaism. Nietzsche advocated a much more radical form of cultural antisemitism, one that was easily combined with the social Darwinist emphasis on the importance of purity of blood and racial survival. Just such a combination can be seen in Houston Stewart Chamberlain's *Foundations of the Nineteenth Century*. In vol. I chapt. 5 ("The Entrance of the Jews into the History of the West")[68] he elaborates at length on the destructive influence of the Jews both racially, by adulterating German blood through interbreeding, and culturally, by infecting Europe with Semitic-Christian values. Unlike Nietzsche, however, Chamberlain sought to solve the latter of these two "problems" not by denying Christianity altogether, but by cleansing it of its supposed Semitic accretions. This was the Aryan Christianity – by no means unique to Chamberlain – called "positive Christianity" by the Nazis. It posited an Aryan Jesus and was thoroughly compatible with racism, imperialism, and exterminatory antisemitism.

What to do with discredited Christianity – to scrap it entirely or to try and salvage something useful from it – was a serious issue, but that European culture had been harmfully influenced by the Jews via orthodox Christianity was widely agreed on. Schopenhauer, Wagner, Chamberlain and many others dealt with this issue, but Nietzsche pursued it with a greater vehemence to a greater degree. Robert Wistrich wrote in *Hitler and the Holocaust*, that "It was the Judaeo-Christian ethic that had alienated mankind from the wholeness of the natural order in pursuit of the 'lie' of a transcendent God. Judaeo-Christianity in its secularized form had, he [Hitler] believed, given birth to contemporary teachings of pacifism, equality before God and the law, human brotherhood, and compassion for the weak, which the Nazis were determined to uproot."[69]

Here at least, if we accept Wistrich's reasonable and balanced summary, Nietzsche and Hitler were in full agreement.

Nietzsche sought a world completely free of Jewish influence. In this world, healthy values of violence and pitiless cruelty without guilt or shame would replace weak and decadent Jewish concepts of moral law, pacifism and democracy. No longer would the weak and sickly dominate their betters with false concepts of right and wrong. The triumph of the slaves, the vulgar, the herd would be overthrown. The weak and the unfit would be exterminated (AC 2), and a new "aristocratic morality" would allow the elite, the nobles, to fully indulge "their awful joy and intense delight in all destruction, in all the ecstasies of victory and cruelty" (GM I, 11). The noblest among timid and domesticated human animals would return to their natural state of the beast of prey, able to engage in "murder, arson, rape, and torture, with bravado and a moral equanimity" (GM I, 11) finally made possible by the elimination of false and weak Jewish-Christian ethics.

Steven Aschheim wrote in *The Nietzsche Legacy in Germany 1890-1990* that, in spite of "Walter Kaufmann's interpretive hegemony" there are some who "have linked the philosopher directly to Naziism's atrocities and its ultimate expression: Auschwitz. The fashionable notion that Nietzsche was not anti-Jewish but anti-Christian, they argue, ignores the fact that what Nietzsche most bitterly detested in Christianity was its Jewish origins."[70] While there is a great deal of cogency in this argument, it is I think more accurate to say that what Nietzsche detested in both Judaism and Christianity were their shared ethical concepts. The rejection of those humane and civilized concepts, as well as hatred towards those who had first introduced them, contributed in no small measure toward the attempt to completely eliminate Jewish influence from Europe, both spiritually and physically.

They are also contributing to increasingly evident social maladies in our own day. The unbridled glorification of self and of one's own will is a very logical (if not inevitable) step from the denial of any higher spiritual entity to which we are rightfully subject. Nietzsche thought that we could attain freedom by denying law and asserting ourselves, even our criminal selves, without let or restraint, but this is far from being a self-evident truth. On the contrary, the divine laws received by Europe through Christianity with its profoundly Jewish influence, were invaluable in creating a balance between individual freedom and social responsibility such as has never been found in most of the rest of the world.

Nietzsche's admirers are eager to defend him, sometimes at all costs, and they have not always been completely candid in their defenses. That war, violence, cruelty and evil were healthy and normal, while kindness, mercy, and self-denial were signs of weakness and decadence, are too often positions of Nietzsche's that are defended by evasions and palliatives. It is somehow claimed that Nietzsche had respect for Jews and for the Bible, when the reverse is the case. He could accept a few individual Jews, and some parts of the Bible pertaining to war and conquest, but in the final analysis he was one of the most extreme and even fanatical opponents of Judaism and of Christianity that ever put pen to paper in the name of philosophy.

Works cited

Aschheim, Steven. *The Nietzsche Legacy in Germany 1890-1990*. Berkeley: University of California Press, 1994.

Berdyaev, Nicolai. *Christian Existentialism: A Berdyaev Anthology*. New York: Harper Torchbooks, 1965.

Bergman, Jerry. *Hitler and the Nazi Darwinian Worldview*. Kitchener, Ontario Canada: Joshua Press, 2014.

Chamberlain, Houston Stewart. *The Foundations of the Nineteenth Century*. Translated by John Lees. (London: John Lane, 1912), accessed November 2, 2015, http://www.hschamberlain.net/grundlagen/division0_index.html.

Conquest, Robert. *Reflections on a Ravaged Century*. New York: W.W. Norton, 2001.

Craig, Gordon. *Germany 1866-1945*. Oxford: Clarendon Press, 1978.

Craig, William Lane. *Reasonable Faith: Christian Truth and Apologetics*. Wheaton, IL: Crossway, 2008.

Ferguson, Niall. *Civilization: The Six Killer Apps of Western Power*. London: Penguin Books, 2012.

Hawking, Stephen and Leonard Mlodinow. *The Grand Design: New Answers to the Ultimate Questions of Life*. London: Bantam Books, 2011.

Heine, Heinrich. *On the History of Religion and Philosophy in Germany*. Translated by Howard Pollack Milgate. Cambridge: Cambridge University Press, 2007.

Hollingdale, R.J. *Nietzsche: The Man and His Philosophy*. Cambridge: Cambridge University Press, 1999.

Johnson, Paul. *Modern Times: The World from the Twenties to the Nineties*. New York: Perennial Classics, 1992.

Kant, Immanuel. *An Answer to the Question "What is Enlightenment?"* London: Penguin Books 2009.

Lloyd-Jones, D.M. *The Puritans: Their Origins and Successors.* Edinburgh: The Banner of Truth Trust, 1987.

Machen, John Gresham. *Christianity and Liberalism.* Charleston, SC: Bibliolife, date not given; reprint of the 1923 edition.

Magee, Bryan. *Wagner and Philosophy.* London: Penguin Books, 2001.

McGrath, Alister. *The Twilight of Atheism: The Rise and Fall of Disbelief in the Modern World.* London: Rider, 2004.

Monod, Jacques. *Chance and Necessity: An Essay on the Natural Philosophy of Modern Biology.* Translated by Austryn Wainhouse. New York: Alfred A. Knopf, 1971.

Montgomery, John W. *In Defense of Martin Luther: Essays by John Warwick Montgomery.* Milwaukee: Northwestern Publishing House, 1970.

Murray, Iain H. *Evangelicalism Divided: A Record of Crucial Change in the Years 1950 to 2000.* Edinburgh: The Banner of Truth Trust, 2000.

Nietzsche, Friedrich. *The Antichrist.* Translated by Anthony M. Ludovici. Amherst, NY: Prometheus Books, 2000.

______. *Beyond Good and Evil: Prelude to a Philosophy of the Future.* Translated by R. J. Hollingdale. London: Penguin Books, 2003.

______. *The Genealogy of Morals.* Translated by Horace B. Samuel. Mineola, NY: Dover Publications, 2003.

Oden, Thomas C. *Requiem: A Lament in Three Movements.* Nashville: Abingdon Press, 1995.

Prager, Dennis and Joseph Telushkin. *Why the Jews? The Reason for Antisemitism.* New York: Touchstone, 2003.

Rubenstein, Richard L. and John K. Roth. *Approaches to Auschwitz: The Holocaust and its Legacy.* Louisville KY: Westminster John Knox Press, 2003.

Sanneh, Lamin. *Whose Religion is Christianity? The Gospel Beyond the West.* Cambridge: William B. Eerdmans Publishing, 2003.

Schaeffer, Francis. *The God Who is There.* Downers Grove, IL: IVP Books, 1982.

________. *The Church at the End of the Twentieth Century.* Wheaton, IL: Crossway Books, 1994.

Schaff, Philip. *History of the Christian Church, Vol. 1: Apostolic Christianity from the Birth of Christ to the Death of St. John A.D. 1-100.* Peabody, Mass: Hendrickson Publishers, 2011.

Schweitzer, Albert. *The Quest of the Historical Jesus: A Critical Study of its Progress from Reimarus to Wrede.* Translated by W. Montgomery. Tarlton, OH: Suzeteo Enterprises, 2011.

Van Til, Cornelius. *The Reformed Pastor and Modern Thought.* Phillipsburg, NJ: Presbyterian and Reformed Publishing Company 1980.

Veith, Gene Edward, Jr. *Modern Fascism: Liquidating the Judeo-Christian Worldview.* St. Louis: Concordia, 1993.

Watson, Peter. *The German Genius: Europe's Third Renaissance, The Second Scientific Revolution, and the Twentieth Century.* New York: Harper Perennial, 2011.

Wells, David F. *No Place for Truth or Whatever Happened to Evangelical Authority?* Grand Rapids, MI: William B. Eerdmans Publishing Company, 1993.

Williams, Stephen N. *The Shadow of the Antichrist: Nietzsche's Critique of Christianity.* Grand Rapids, MI: Baker Academic, and Milton Keynes, UK: Paternoster, 2006.

Wistrich, Robert S. *Hitler and the Holocaust.* New York: Modern Library, 2003.

Endnotes

[1] Stephen Hawking and Leonard Mlodinow, *The Grand Design: New Answers to the Ultimate Questions of Life* (London: Bantam Books, 2011), p. 168. The exact size, according to Hawking, was "a billion-trillion-trillionth of a centimeter." He has not informed us how many angels can dance on the head of a pin.

[2] Niall Ferguson, *Civilization: The Six Killer Apps of Western Power* (London: Penguin Books, 2012), p. xv.

[3] Ibid., p. 67, 263.

[4] Lamin Sanneh, *Whose Religion is Christianity? The Gospel Beyond the West* (Cambridge: William B. Eerdmans Publishing, 2003), see especially chapter 2 ("Christianity Reappropriated: The Bible and Its Mother Tongue Variations").

[5] Richard L. Rubenstein and John K. Roth, *Approaches to Auschwitz: The Holocaust and its Legacy* (Louisville KY: Westminster John Knox Press, 2003), p. 57.

[6] David F. Wells, *No Place for Truth or Whatever Happened to Evangelical Authority?* (Grand Rapids, MI: William B. Eerdmans Publishing Company, 1993), p. 88.

[7] Robert S. Wistrich, *Hitler and the Holocaust* (New York: Modern Library, 2003), p. 13.

[8] John W. Montgomery, *In Defense of Martin Luther: Essays by John Warwick Montgomery* (Milwaukee: Northwestern Publishing House, 1970), chapter 2 "Luther and Science."

[9] Jacques Monod, *Chance and Necessity: An Essay on the Natural Philosophy of Modern Biology*, trans. Austryn Wainhouse (New York: Alfred A. Knopf, 1971), p. 174. Monod thinks this was "perhaps" and "in part" due to the Church's distinction between the sacred and the profane, meaning that the mysteries of nature were not sacred and off-limits, but open to investigation.

[10] Ferguson, *Civilization*, p. 287, all quotes.

[11] Philip Schaff, *History of the Christian Church (vol. 1, Apostolic Christianity from the Birth of Christ to the Death of St. John A.D. 1-100)* (Peabody, Mass: Hendrickson Publishers, 2011), p. 741.

[12] D.M. Lloyd-Jones, *The Puritans: Their Origins and Successors* (Edinburgh: The Banner of Truth Trust, 1987), p. 218.

[13] Prager, Dennis Prager and Joseph Telushkin, *Why the Jews? The Reason for Antisemitism* (New York / London: Touchstone, 2003), p. 202

[14] Francis Schaeffer, *The God Who is There* (Downers Grove, IL: IVP Books, 1982), p. 108.

[15] Adolf Hitler, *Mein Kampf*, trans. Ralph Manheim (Boston: Houghton Mifflin, 1999), p. 306.

[16] See Prager and Telushkin, *Why the Jews?* chapters 10 ("Secular Antisemitism: The Enlightenment") and 11 ("Leftist Antisemitism"). That people can totally reject the Bible yet still hate Jews for other reasons is too hard for some people to grasp.

[17] Robert Conquest, *Reflections on a Ravaged Century* (New York: W.W. Norton, 2001), pp. 40, 51-52, 55.

[18] Paul Johnson, *Modern Times: The World from the Twenties to the Nineties* (New York: Perennial Classics, 1992), p. 579.

[19] Nicolai Berdyaev, *Christian Existentialism: A Berdyaev Anthology*, (New York: Harper Torchbooks, 1965), p. 196.

[20] Johnson, *Modern Times*, p. 64. Johnson even admits that Marx recognized the necessity of and advocated the use of "revolutionary terror" to destroy the old society and establish the new, and quotes Marx to this effect (p. 66).

[21] Thomas C. Oden, *Requiem: A Lament in Three Movements*, (Nashville: Abingdon Press, 1995), p. 126.

[22] Peter Watson, *The German Genius: Europe's Third Renaissance, The Second Scientific Revolution, and the Twentieth Century* (New York: Harper Perennial, 2011), pp. 45-47.

[23] William Lane Craig, *Reasonable Faith: Christian Truth and Apologetics* (Wheaton, IL: Crossway, 2008), p. 342.

[24] Watson, *German Genius*, pp. 421-422 (both for the quote and for comments on the conflict of loyalty that follow).

[25] Schaff, *History of the Christian Church*, pp. 856, 858.

[26] Francis Schaeffer, *The Church at the End of the Twentieth Century* (Wheaton, IL: Crossway Books, 1994), p. 110.

[27] Ibid., p. 111.

[28] Ibid., pp. 110-111.

[29] John Gresham Machen, *Christianity and Liberalism* (Charleston, SC: Bibliolife, date not given, reprint of the 1923 edition), p. 2.

[30] Craig, *Reasonable Faith*, p. 347.

[31] Schaeffer, *The Church at the End of the Twentieth Century*, p. 115 (both quotes).

[32] Alister McGrath, *The Twilight of Atheism: The Rise and Fall of Disbelief in the Modern World* (London: Rider, 2004), p. 49.

[33] Ibid.

[34] I hope to be able to describe elsewhere Kant's political authoritarianism, elitism, philosophical indifference to human suffering, and new forms of antisemitism, and to show that he articulated some potentially fascist trends albeit in embryonic form.

[35] Watson, *German Genius*, p. 56.

[36] Ibid., p. 198. The comparison to Hitler is mine, not Watson's.

[37] Ibid., p. 43.

[38] Ibid., pp. 107, 93.

[39] Stephen N. Williams, *The Shadow of the Antichrist: Nietzsche's Critique of Christianity* (Grand Rapids, MI: Baker Academic, and Milton Keynes, UK: Paternoster, 2006), p. 31 [citing Hegel, *Early Theological Writings* (Chicago, 1948), pp. 325-36].

[40] R. J. Hollingdale, *Nietzsche: The Man and His Philosophy,* (Cambridge: Cambridge University Press, 1999), p. 19.

[41] Heinrich Heine, *On the History of Religion and Philosophy in Germany*, trans. Howard Pollack Milgate (Cambridge: Cambridge University Press, 2007), p. 115 (all quotes in this paragraph).

[42] Watson, *German Genius*, p. 109 (both quotes in this paragraph).

[43] Gordon Craig, *Germany 1866-1945* (Oxford: Clarendon Press, 1978), pp. 190, 194-197.

[44] Ibid., p. 82.

[45] Watson, *German Genius*, Part IV chapters 31 & 32.

[46] Gene Edward Veith, Jr. *Modern Fascism: Liquidating the Judeo-Christian Worldview* (St. Louis: Concordia, 1993), pp. 143-144.

[47] Immanuel Kant, *An Answer to the Question "What is Enlightenment?"* (London: Penguin Books 2009), pp. 4-5.

[48] Veith, *Modern Fascism*, p. 53. He says "weakened" when "denied" or "nullified" would be more accurate, in my opinion.

[49] Philip Schaff, *History of the Christian Church, Vol. 1: Apostolic Christianity from the Birth of Christ to the Death of St John A.D. 1-100* (Peabody, Mass.: Hendrickson Publishers, 2011), p. 208.

[50] Cornelius Van Til, *The Reformed Pastor and Modern Thought* (Phillipsburg, NJ: Presbyterian and Reformed Publishing Company 1980), p. 106.

[51] For examples of Christian pastors who believed in Darwinism see Jerry Bergman's *Hitler and the Nazi Darwinian Worldview,* (Kitchener, Ontario Canada: Joshua Press, 2014).

[52] Albert Schweitzer, *The Quest of the Historical Jesus: A Critical Study of its Progress from Reimarus to Wrede*, trans. W. Montgomery, (Tarlton, OH: Suzeteo Enterprises, 2011), p. 109.

[53] Ibid., p. 78.

[54] Craig, *Germany 1866-1945*, p. 181

[55] Schweitzer, The Quest of the Historical Jesus, p. 103.

[56] Ibid., pp. 103-104 (both quotes).

[57] Bryan Magee, *Wagner and Philosophy* (London: Penguin Books, 2001), p. 160 (all quotes).

[58] Schaff, *History of the Christian Church*, p. 409. He adds that this concept was followed by "the whole Tübingen School."

[59] Iain H. Murray, *Evangelicalism Divided: A Record of Crucial Change in the Years 1950 to 2000* (Edinburgh: The Banner of Truth Trust, 2000), pp. 270-271.

[60] Craig, *Germany 1866-1945*, p. 181 (all quotes).

[61] Thomas Oden, *Requiem: A Lament in Three Movements* (Nashville: Abingdon Press, 1995), pp. 109, 48, 27.

[62] Craig, *Germany 1866-1945*, p. 182 (both quotes).

[63] Ibid., pp. 182-183.

[64] Friedrich Nietzsche, *The Genealogy of Morals*, trans. Horace B. Samuel (Mineola, NY: Dover Publications, 2003), 105.

[65] Friedrich Nietzsche, *The Antichrist*, trans. Anthony M. Ludovici (Amherst, NY: Prometheus Books, 2000), 34.

[66] Friedrich Nietzsche, *Beyond Good and Evil: Prelude to a Philosophy of the Future*, trans. R. J. Hollingdale (London: Penguin Books, 2003), 182.

[67] Adolf Hitler, *Mein Kampf*, trans. Ralph Manheim (Boston: Houghton Mifflin, 1999), 300.

[68] Houston Stewart Chamberlain, *The Foundations of the Nineteenth Century*, trans. John Lees (London: John Lane, 1912), accessed November 2, 2015, http://www.hschamberlain.net/grundlagen/division0_index.html

[69] Robert Wistrich, *Hitler and the Holocaust* (New York: Modern Library, 2003), 132, 135.

[70] Steven Aschheim, *The Nietzsche Legacy in Germany 1890-1990* (Berkeley: University of California Press, 1994), 327.

Don't miss out!

Visit the website below and you can sign up to receive emails whenever Joseph E. Keysor publishes a new book. There's no charge and no obligation.

https://books2read.com/r/B-A-QOAX-JSZQB

BOOKS2READ

Connecting independent readers to independent writers.

About the Author

The author was born in 1952 in Evanston Illinois. He has a BA and a Masters and has worked as an English teacher for over twenty-five years in Asia (mainland China) and the Middle East (Oman and Saudi Arabia).